Learn H
Full Time eBay Reselling
Business

10 Manuscripts

Learn How to Sell on eBay Full Time With These Secrets

Included Books

Thrift Store Champ VS. Garage Sale Superstar

Turning Thrift Store Oddities And Rarities Into Cool Cash

Turning Thrift Store Electronics And Gadgets Into Cash Magic

Turning Thrift Store Vintage Toys Into Stacks Of Cash

Reseller Secrets To Dominating A Thrift Store Revealed

Instagram Marketing Secrets Revealed

Turning Thrift Store Clothing Into Cash

Thrift Store Reselling Secrets You Wish You Knew

Thrifting And Winning

Thrift Store Knick Knacks Into Giant Cash Stacks

Table of Contents

Book 1: Thrift Store Champ VS. Garage Sale Supertar

Book 2: Turning Thrift Store Oddities And Rarities Into Cool Cash

Book 3: Turning Thrift Store Electronics And Gadgets Into Cash Magic

Book 4: Turning Thrift Store Vintage Toys Into Stacks Of Cash

Book 5: Reseller Secrets To Dominating A Thrift Store Revealed

Book 6: Instagram Marketing Secrets Revealed

Book 7: Turning Thrift Store Clothing Into Cash

Book 8: Thrift Store Reselling Secrets You Wish You Knew

Book 9: Thrifting And Winning

Book 10: Thrift Store Knick Knacks Into Giant Cash Stacks

THRIFT STORE CHAMP VS. GARAGE SALE SUPERSTAR

50 UNIQUE AND COLLECTIBLE ITEMS YOU CAN BUY AT THRIFT STORES AND GARAGE SALES TO RESELL ON EBAY AND AMAZON

RICK RILEY

Introduction

This book contains proven steps and strategies on how to find unique and collectable items that are worth big money when resold online. If you haven't been to a garage sale for a while, you might wonder what people really do sell. The phrase that one person's junk is another person's treasure can prove all too true when looking through the random offerings set before you. Do you know how to get the best price possible for the item you want? Does the seller have any idea how much the item is really worth? By taking a good look at what types of items can be sold for a great profit and what is merely junk, you will be prepared at any garage sale.

Garage sales and thrift stores have a plethora of different items that are simply waiting for the right buyer. However, most people don't know what items can be resold online for a nice profit. By taking a look at the items that are most unique and collectable, you will be able to pick them out amongst the clutter of a garage sale table or thrift store shelf. So, let's take a look at what to look for when you step into that garage sale or thrift store! It might amaze you what you have been missing in the past!

Chapter 1- Which Items are Unique at Garage Sales?

Most of us have probably been to a garage sale before. It seems as though the junk that the homeowner no longer wants clutters collapsible tables and blankets on the ground. With your initial glance, you notice old clothing, games with missing pieces, and maybe some toys that have been a little too loved. The same can be said of the items you encounter on a thrift store shelf. Is it just junk, or are there other possibilities amongst the clutter? Is there anything at all here that can be useful to you or others?

By knowing what to look for when you step into this hodge podge of junk will make the experience a little less overwhelming and a little more calming. Despite that fact that the operator of the garage sale only aims to declutter his or her home, the offerings might have a little more value than one realizes. In the end, a garage sale has one goal: to get rid of unnecessary goods. If you offer the operator a decent price, chances are that you can walk away with a unique item that can be resold online at a nice profit.

If you're new to the garage sale scene, try looking for these unique items when strolling along!

Musical instruments

People will often sell old instruments at garage sales. Even if they're in disrepair, you can easily take them in for repairs and resell them for a profit. Many an unsuspecting garage sale operator will put out their children's used school band instruments and just want to get rid of them. Let their loss be your gain.

Tools

Look for high quality brands and tools that you might not find in too many places. If they look older, don't be afraid to pick them up. If they're the right price, you might find that they're worth even more later on.

Electronics

People are often leery of buying electronics at a garage sale. Most of the time, the item might not even work anymore and you can be taken for a ride. However, if the seller wants to sell it bad enough, he or she will allow you to test the item prior to purchase. Look for electronics that you might not see too often, such as calculator watches or hand held video games.

DVDs and other media

Look for rare movies, VHS tapes, cassettes and other items that you don't see very much of anymore. Chances are, there is someone out there who is looking for them. I like to look for CDs and other music that I can try to resell. It's especially nice to be able to pick up items that are near new condition. If they're rare and in great condition, chances are that I can get a good price when I resell them.

Textbooks

You might not know if these are good for resale until after you purchase them. I usually pick them up anyway because I find that I would rather waste a few dollars if they are potentially worth more. When looking at text books, I look at their ages, topics, and condition to see if they might be a good item for resale. If they're too outdated, then they might be collectable.

You don't know unless you try!

Automobile parts

If you should come across automobile parts at a garage sale, ask what model of car they come from. If it is an older model car, it might be worth picking up the parts. Some older parts are harder to find and that could mean a little extra money in your pocket.

Clothing

Looking through garage sale clothing can be a drag. For many years, if I saw that a garage sale boasted mostly clothing, I would hit the gas and keep going. However, try taking a look through the offerings. There might be designer names, sports teams, or other factors that can make the clothing worth more than the seller thinks.

Toys

Toys at a garage sale can either be sink or swim. It all depends on how used the toys are. Take a look through the toys and see if you can find some that are not typical to the normal offerings. If they look different and you haven't seen them before, it might be a good investment to see where they came from and what they're worth. If the toys seem to be in poor shape and cannot be cleaned up, then walk away.

Art

Old pictures and paintings are another good purchase to resell. Since people have vastly different tastes in art, it is likely that you can sell the artwork online for what you want in terms of price. You never know, you might find a valuable piece that is worth millions!

Furniture

Many people are reluctant to buy furniture at garage sales. This is especially true if it is upholstered. However, there might be a profitable find amongst garage sale furniture. Take a closer look to see if the furniture is unique, in good shape, and whether or not you can resell the item. The more unique the piece, the better the chances of fetching a good price for its resale.

Don't turn away because you consider it ugly. Beauty might be in the eye of another beholder!

Jewelry

Most of the time, the jewelry at a garage sale tends to be small pieces dumped in a shoe box for you to look through. Don't be afraid to take the time to look, though. In that box might be jewelry that is antique, made of precious metal or stones, or unique enough that you can resell it for much more than you are buying it for. Often times, people have no idea what treasures they are throwing out when they clean house for a garage sale.

Bikes and Scooters

Another offering that I tend to see at garage sales are bikes and scooters. A lot of the time, the owners don't ride them and they just take up unnecessary room in the garage. It could be to your gain though to pick them up. Take a look at the build and the make of the bike or scooter. If it's of good quality, chances are that you can sell it for much more online.

Sports equipment

Sports equipment is another area that can be worth your time to look through. Depending on the season, people might be getting rid of some valuable sporting equipment to make space for new items. Take a look at items such as skis, baseball equipment, and golfing equipment to see if you can find articles that can be resold.

Kitchen Utensils

It might gross you out to look through kitchen utensils at a garage sale, but this is another area that can yield some pretty good profits. Even if they're not the cleanest, they can always be cleaned up before reselling. Look at the silverware, china, and other items that stand out to you. If it's not an item you have seen too often, it doesn't hurt to buy it if it's priced right!

Exercise equipment

Looking through exercise equipment can be a good way to find something that can be resold. Items such as hand weights, weightlifting benches, and medicine balls can all be resold for a profit. If they have exercise machines, all the better. Depending on the shape and the type of the machine, you can find a buyer who is willing to put their money into your hands for it.

When looking at items at a garage sale or a thrift store, really look for items that jump out at you. If they catch your attention, they might catch the attention of potential buyers online. Remember, you are not looking for items to suit your tastes, but items that can be resold for a profit. If you think that you can turn and resell this item for more than you're buying it for, then it is a decent investment.

Sometimes you will know when the item before you has more value than what the operator is selling it for. Don't be afraid to purchase it. Their loss is your gain. They will just be grateful to get rid of the items. Overall, a garage sale or thrift store is a prime place to find other peoples' throw outs to make yourself a nice profit!

Chapter 2- Which Items are Collectable?

Garage sale and thrift store items can hold surprises you never would think you could find here. I have seen countless stories of people finding items on garage sales and thrift stores that ended up being worth thousands, even millions, of dollars. How can this happen? It's simple. People throw garage sales to get rid of unwanted items and have a little extra cash in their pockets. When they go through their home clearing out these items, their overall value can oftentimes be overlooked. This means that there is tons of potential wealth at your fingertips!

There are tons of items that people collect that can easily be gathered at a garage sale or at a thrift store. Collectables can be anything from a salt and pepper shaker set from Disney World to a set of playing cards. People collect almost anything. Keep this in mind as you look through the sale. In this chapter, I'm going to point out some of the top collectable items that you might find at a typical garage sale or on a thrift store shelf.

Jewelry

We touched a little bit upon jewelry as being a unique garage sale item in the last chapter. Jewelry can also be a collectible item. Items that boast characters, different types of stones, and different brands might be something worth buying.

Rare and Themed Furniture

Different types of furniture can also be consider collectible in the right circumstances. When looking at it from a collector's point of view, try seeing if it could be a part of a larger set, if it's made of a certain material, and whether it too might have a theme that could be collected. Some children's furniture is often themed after cartoons and fairy tales. This could be a great selling point to a potential buyer.

Artwork and Pictures

If you have good eye for fine art, then look through what they have at a sale. Some pieces are very valuable and collectable. Be aware, however. A lot of fine art and pictures are knock offs of the real thing. Be sure you know if it's the real deal before you sell it as such. However, you might just have a great find in your hands. At the right price, either is good!

Kitchen utensils

I was reading an article about a woman who bought a bowl at a garage sale for three dollars and found out that it was a priceless antique. She merely liked the look of the bowl. The same can be said of other kitchen accessories. Themed glasses from restaurants, plates from a certain cartoon, and glassware that catches the eye are a few good leads to finding kitchen utensils that might be worth more to someone than the few dollars you will spend on it.

Pottery

When looking at pottery at a garage sale, take a look at the piece from a collector's perspective. See if it has a marking to tell you whether it has been massed produced or is a part of a limited collection. Just because you feel it might not be pretty doesn't mean that it's not valuable. Make sure that there is not any significant damage that would make it worthless. If you feel that there is something unique about the piece, don't be afraid to buy it if it's priced right.

Trading Cards

Trading cards are a huge opportunity at garage sales. From baseball cards to card games such as Pokémon, you can find cards that are worth much more than what the garage sale is selling if for. Most often, they are sold in packets of many, so pick them up and look through them later. There might be one out of a hundred cards that can make you some money.

Music, Movies, Books and Magazines

We covered unique media in the last chapter, but there is another opportunity to be found among media at a garage sale. Think Walt Disney. A lot of the Disney movies have been put into the "vault" and will only be released every ten years. This being said, look for old VHS, DVD and other media dealing with Disney. They can be worth your while if they're in good shape.

Other forms of collectable media can be found in older children's books, antique books, and old magazines. Older media often are limited and can be worth money when resold. Don't bypass a pile of magazines. There might be a few in there that will definitely be worth the money.

Knick Knacks

Look at the offerings of figurines and statues when at a garage sale. Some of these are collectible and quite valuable. Take a look at the condition, the stamp on the bottom, or other elements that could mark this item as something more than just a pretty ornament.

Precious metals and stones

Along with jewelry, take a look for precious metals and stones. The jewelry itself might be shot, but the elements of it can be resold for profit. On items such as rings, take a look at the engraving in the band. It will tell you the quantity of metal, such as gold, that is found in it. Items made of sterling silver can also be of great value. Depending on the density of the metal, you might be holding money in your hands!

Vintage items

Vintage items, such as stuffed animals, toys, and figurines show up all the time at garage sales. Take a close look at everything and if you believe that it is vintage or an original, pick it up. You never know what can be lurking in the piles of stuff!

Coins

Old coins are highly collectible. However, you really need to take a look at the condition that the coin is in and whether or not it can be cleaned up. The older the coins, the better the chance that they are worth something. I once found a coin that was dated around the time of the Civil War amongst a small bag of coins for sale. It was actually worth quite a bit and once it was cleaned up, it had very little damage on it.

Old toys

Wooden toys and heavy plastic toys are a good sign that they are older. The toy companies don't use these materials as much anymore, so you know when you find something that looks like it's made of these materials, it is often older. People will collect these items for memories as well as value.

Think of the toys that you had as a child. Barbies, My Little Ponies, and the old Teenaged Mutant Ninja Turtle dolls are all worth money now. If it seems like it is an original or from the time period when the toy came out, snatch it up!

Sports memorabilia

Sportsman like to sign their names to things. For example, baseballs, prints, and jerseys are all hot items that sports stars autograph. The older the autograph and the greater the popularity of the sports star, the greater the likelihood that it might be worth money. If you know the player and know of the item's value, buy it. People collect sports memorabilia and are constantly looking for different additions to their collections.

Handbags

Certain brands of handbags are highly popular and collectable. Take a good look at handbags that you believe might be of higher quality. Be sure to look at the quality of the bag, whether or not it has any damage, and if it has a good label. Certain styles can also be highly collectible.

Fast food toys

If I had known that all of the toys that I had gotten from my Happy Meal would be worth money today, I would have held on to them. Yes, there are people out there who collect old fast food toys! The better the shape, the more in demand they are. If they're still in original packaging, even better!

Just because you wouldn't think of an item as a collectable does not mean that it isn't. There are many types of collectors out there. This chapter just covers that most popular items that you can find at a garage sale or thrift store. By being aware of what can be sold as a collectable, you can find some great and even unusual finds at thrift stores and garage sales!

Chapter 3- Other Money Makers

Remember, there are tons of possibilities to be had at a garage sale or a thrift store. Just because it might not be worth much to you doesn't mean that someone else out there isn't looking for that particular item! Be aware and be ready to put your money into something that can be turned into profit.

While the item itself might not be worth anything, you might find that what the item is made of or how it is packaged can make a great difference when it comes to resale. In this chapter, we are going to take a look at other items that can be turned into a profit from a garage sale or a thrift store.

Scrap metal

Look for metals such as aluminum, copper, and steel. Even if the item isn't worth anything as an item, the metal it is made out of can be resold for different uses.

New and unopened packages

I have found that people will buy just about anything if it's priced right. Often times, these items are stored without even being opened. These end up being donated or sold on garage sales. Depending on the item, you might have a great find at a fraction of the price you can sell it for online.

Used clothing

Depending on the style and the brand, clothing found at garage sales and in thrift stores can be resold online for a profit. Try looking for sizes that are not average, such as extra small to very large sizes. These are often in higher demand than items that you can find anywhere. Make sure that the articles of clothing are stain free and don't have any tears.

Video games and systems

Video games and systems can be turned into a good profit. The older systems that are no longer manufactured can be sold online for a significant amount of money. The games that go with the systems can be sold for a profit as well. Even if the game system is still being manufactured, you can still find games that are rare. Use your scrutinizing eyes to see if you think that these will be great items to resell.

Linens

Linens that have unique designs and details can be a great item to resell. However, you really need to look over them carefully before purchase to ensure that there aren't any stains or tears in them.

Designer items

Items that are fashionable and have a good brand on them can easily be resold for more than you will pay at a garage sale. Take a close look at the labels and the craftsmanship before purchasing these because there are many knock-off items out there.

Records

Along with media, records are a great purchase from a garage sale or thrift store. Just be careful to check for scratches!

Picture Frames

Picture frames can often be resold for a profit. The more detailed the frame the better. Also, look at the material that the frame is made of. Some picture frames are older and can be considered collectable and valuable.

If you're in doubt as to what you can sell online, visit the sites themselves and browse through the items that other sellers have listed. You might be surprised at what can be resold that you can find at a local garage sale or thrift store! If in doubt and the price is low enough, go ahead and buy it and check on it later.

You may not know the true value of an item until you get it home and take a closer look at it. Just be conscientious of what you're spending and whether or not you're making a good investment. In the next chapter, I'm going to give you some pointers and tips on how to look for garage sales. Once you know how to plan a day of garage sales, then we can look at how to make sure you're getting a good price.

Chapter 4- Tips for Finding Garage Sales

In the summer time, garage sales are a dime a dozen. Everyone seems to be throwing one. How do you make sure that you're finding ones that will produce the greatest chance of finding quality items? You really never know, but learning to time your garage sale shopping and the routes that you take can help you get the maximum time out of your garage sale venture.

Use your resources

You want to make sure that you can visit the maximum amount of sales in a day. The more you hit up, the better chance you have of finding items for resale. Before you even leave your home, take some time to plan out your route. Get a copy of the newspaper or search online on websites such as Craigslist for a listing of garage sales for that day or weekend. Find ones that would be feasible for you to visit.

When driving to a sale that you have seen listed, don't drive by the unlisted ones. People may not list their garage sales in the paper, so you might not know they're there until you drive past them. Remember, every garage sale is an opportunity. Stop in and see what it has to offer!

Start Early

This might irritate those who set up the sales, but if you're one of the first customers, you stand a higher likelihood of getting the good items first. The sellers might not be as willing to negotiate the price, but if you find something that you are certain that you can resell for a good profit, it's better to find it early and get it before someone else does.

Community Garage Sales

It has become a common practice for neighborhoods to hold garage sales on the same day. This means that you can find the maximum number of sales without driving too far. These sales are often advertised in advance, so if you know when the community garage sale is to be held, you can plan on hitting it early and still have time to visit other sales.

Look at What They are Offering

When looking at an advertisement for a garage sale, look at the items that the seller is highlighting. This can often give you a clue as to the type and quality of items you are going to find there. It might not always be true, but I have found that garage sales often have items consistent with the larger ones for sale.

One good rule is to never pass up a garage sale. Even if you feel that all they have to offer is junk, you might be missing a pleasant and profitable surprise. When people throw garage sales, they don't think about the overall value of what they're selling. The just want to get rid of it. Which brings me to my next topic. You will want to make sure you get a good and reasonable price when shopping garage sales. You must learn to haggle.

Chapter 5- How to Haggle for the Best Price

As mentioned before, a garage sale is a method that people use to make some extra money off of their unwanted things. The goal for them is to get rid of as much of it as they can so that they don't have to donate or store it again. This means that those who operate garage sales are often more willing to negotiate the price that they set on an item.

Garage sales now operate on the "make me an offer" method. The person operating the sale doesn't place price tags on them but allows those who are interested in buying them to make an offer on the item. The seller has a good idea of what they would like to get out of it, but if the buyer wants to offer more, then that is acceptable as well.

What you need to know is how to get a price that you're willing to pay and still be able to get a good profit out of the item. This process is called haggling, and you can often get great deals by bargaining with the seller a little bit. Let's take a look at some tips to help you get the best price out of items using this method.

Start Low

In your mind, you probably have a good idea of what you will be willing to pay for the item. The seller has an idea in his or her mind what they would like to sell if for. So, start low and see if you can get the seller to bite at a lower price than you hope to obtain the item for. If the seller knows the true worth of the item, they will give you a counter offer. If it sounds reasonable, you can take it, or you can continue to bargain with the seller. If the seller has too high of a price expectation, leave it behind.

Work the Price Up

If the seller won't take your first offer, try raising it at small increments. Try moving it up by five, ten, or twenty-five cents. Once the seller sees that you're willing to negotiate, he or she will play the game with you.

Pretend to Lose Interest

If the haggling gets too much, pretend that you're giving up on the item. If the seller wants to get rid of it bad enough, they will be willing to give you the item at the last price you mentioned. Make sure that this last price is near what you expect to pay or lower.

Have a Friendly Conversation with the Seller

If you start out the experience by chatting with the seller, you are more likely to get what you want at the price you want. Try going up to the seller and making small talk. Once you're ready to purchase, it will be easier to work the price down on the items you want to purchase.

Make sure that you are shopping garage sales as a seasoned shopper. If you know what you want and how much you're willing to spend, then it will be easier to negotiate prices with the people running the sale. If it's later in the day, the seller will probably be more willing to part with the item for any price, so be aware of the time of day and the temperament of the seller.

In thrift stores, you won't need the ability to haggle. To get good prices, look for sales, coupons and other methods to save money. Sometimes, if you ask for a bulk discount, the cashier is more than willing to give you one. It never hurts to try. Look for days when there are sales, but make sure that the store isn't too crowded. The more crowded the store, the harder it's going to be to find items you can sell.

Thrift stores often give you coupons for donating to them. If you have purchased items that you cannot sell, donate them again just for the coupon. The coupon is often for about twenty percent, which could be a great savings if you have a lot of merchandise.

Whether you are searching for your items at thrift stores or at garage sales, learn how to get the best price possible so that you can achieve the maximum profit from you item. I prefer to go to garage sales in the summer because I can get better deals from the sellers. In the winter, thrift stores help me maintain my inventory. Do whatever works for you. It might be a combination of both.

Chapter 6- Knowing When to Buy and When to Step Away

People often struggle when it comes to knowing when the sale is going foul. A bidding war isn't something that you want to carry out for too long. There is a time to know when to step away and move on. Unless you know the item is absolutely valuable, it's okay to step away and continue on your route. In this chapter, I'm going to give you some tips on knowing when to stay and when to go.

The Item is Valuable

You know that the item that you hold in your hands can be resold at a great profit. However, the seller knows it as well. He wants to get rid of it, but he won't let it go for under a certain price. This is when you really need to think about your profit margin. If you cannot get much more out of it than what you're buying it for, then it's okay to walk away. On the other hand, if you know that you can make a lot of money off of it, it might be good to just give in to the seller and pay a little more than you planned for it.

The Item is Damaged

You could potentially make a good profit from the item. However, there is a damaged spot that will decrease its resale value. This is where you need to evaluate whether or not you can repair and resell the item, sell it as is, or leave it for someone else. Sometimes, you can fix the damages on used items and resell them for a good profit. Really think about this as you haggle the price. Since it is being sold damaged, you might be able to get a better price for it when this detail is presented to the seller.

The Seller is Asking Too Much

Let's face it. People have grand ideas in their heads about what they think they should be able to sell a certain item for. The item might be purchased for just as much new. Take this into account when shopping at garage sales. Even if it's in near new condition, it's not new and you shouldn't be required to pay a new price for it. If the seller isn't willing to bargain, walk away.

Knowing when the bargaining isn't working is a good way to gauge whether or not you need to keep trying or walk away. Once you've haggled a few times, you will know when a seller is going to give in or if the whole thing is a waste of time. Just remember to not pay more than you believe is reasonable for the item. You both want to make money, but you want to be in a position where you can maximize your profit.

Chapter 7- Sealing the Deal and Making Your Profit

Once you've haggled a good price for the items that you're interested in buying, it's time to close the sale. By doing it the right way, you will make both yourself and the seller feel better about the transaction. After all, you're not trying to take advantage of the other person, but you also don't want to be taken advantage of.

Make the entire process as friendly as possible. Treat the seller the way that you want to be treated. If you treat them like they're stupid, then they won't be as willing to sell to you. You want to have an enjoyable and friendly experience. Once you have settled on a price, pay promptly and thank the seller. If you should return for another garage sale put on by the same seller, they might remember the way you acted the last time you visited.

When you're loading your purchases in your vehicle, make sure that you're putting them in a place that won't cause them damage. You don't want to ruin your items before you have a chance to sell them. Make sure you have packing items in your car just in case. Tissue paper, boxes and other items that will make it easier to transport your purchases will ensure that you get them home in the same condition you purchased them in.

You ultimately want to make sure that you're giving you online customer the same item that you purchased yourself, if not in better shape. You might have to do some minor repairs and cleaning to your purchases in order to make them worth more when selling them online. Even though you have to put in a little extra work, it is often worth it when you receive the profit you hoped for.

In your home, you also want to make sure that they are put in a place where they cannot be damaged. Take good care of your purchases so that you will be able to get the best price out of them once you list them online. If you don't have seller accounts, then now is a good time to create them. Just follow the steps on the website you hope to sell on.

After you have taken good pictures of your items, you can list them on Amazon or eBay and see how much of a profit you are going to make for your efforts. You might be surprised at the sale prices of some of the items that sell on these websites.

You're well on your way to finding garage sale and thrift store items that can be resold for profits on Amazon and eBay. As you get used to the process, you will find new methods and techniques that will help you make a good profit. Good luck on your adventure and I wish you profit and success!

Conclusion

I hope this book was able to help you to learn how to shop at garage sales and find items that can be resold for profit. Both garage sales and thrift stores are a treasure chest of goods. Some may be junk, but others can be resold for good profits. By knowing what to look for and how to get them at a good price, you're well on your way to becoming a profit-earning seller!

The next step is to try going to garage sales and thrift stores and searching for items that can be resold. If you're going to a garage sale, try haggling the prices with the seller to get the best possible price for the item that you hope to resell. Just remember that your goal is to make a profit by reselling items online. Don't pay too much!

TURNING THRIFT STORE ODDITIES AND RARITIES INTO COOL CASH

50 OFF THE WALL ITEMS YOU CAN BUY CHEAP AT THRIFT STORES AND RESELL ON EBAY AND AMAZON FOR HUGE PROFIT

RICK RILEY

Introduction

I want to thank you for purchasing the book, Turning Thrift Store Oddities And Rarities Into Cool Cash: 50 Off The Wall Items You Can Buy Cheap At Thrift Stores And Resell On eBay And Amazon For Huge Profit.

This book contains proven steps and strategies on how to take the oddities that you will find in thrift stores and sell them for a profit on Amazon and eBay.

This book is unlike any other book you will find that teaches you how to make money on Amazon and eBay. Most books will tell you about all of the most popular items that you can sell on the sites but that still leaves you with a ton of competition. Other people trying to start their own businesses flipping items they have found at thrift stores.

This book on the other hand is going to teach you how to take those oddities that you will find at thrift stores and flip them for a profit. The items that other flippers would not think of purchasing and reselling, the items that are so often overlooked but sell for a great profit!

This book will help you understand which oddities are going to sell the best and what you need to do to make sure that they reach the right buyers. You will also learn a few selling secrets along the way. I hope you enjoy the book and I hope that it helps you to understand what oddities you will be able to make a profit from.

Thanks again for purchasing this book, I hope you enjoy it!

Chapter 1
Strange Finds You Can Profit From

So many people are going to thrift stores and resale shops looking for the best items to sell online. This means that they usually overlook the strange items that you can find and sell for a huge profit. Most of the time people are focused on clothing, antiques and the obvious items that can be found and resold. However, in this chapter you are going to learn about the odd items you can find in thrift stores and sell for a profit.

1. Crazy cat lady figurines. Yes, crazy cat figurines! And no, I am not talking about going out and purchasing 30 tiny cat figurines. There are actually Crazy cat lady action figures that come with several different types of cats. These can be found randomly at thrift stores and they sell very quickly on eBay and Amazon.

2. Miniature log caskets with skeleton. This is a very strange item that people really love to purchase and it is simply a miniature of an old fashioned casket carved out of a piece of wood. Inside the casket you will find a small carved skeleton. Many of these are handmade by random, unknown people and then for whatever reason they end up being donated to thrift stores where they can sell for anywhere from a quarter to fifty cents. Sometimes even less. They can be re-sold very quickly for about $40, depending on the style, with some versions going for even more.

3. Broken vintage and collectible electronics are another odd item that you wouldn't normally think could be re-sold but they are. If you have any type of broken electronics lying around your house that you can no

longer use, just don't have time to fix or don't know how, there is always someone out there looking for these types of items. You can find broken electronics at thrift stores and purchase them for literally pennies and sometimes they will even give these to you. List them and watch them fly off of your virtual shelves.

4. Another highly unusual item that you never would expect to sell are shoes with a sole filled with different random items. They can be filled with glitter, small stones, gems or even tiny doll parts. If you find these at your thrift store make sure to pick them up! I'm seen them sell for up to about $50 a pair. I am not going to claim to know why these items sell but the fact is that they do sell. It may be because they are rare or it could just be that people like the way they look.

5. I honestly cannot explain why this next item would ever sell but it does. Pictures/photos of animals wearing human clothing and taking part in their everyday life. The photos/pictures depict animals doing things such as dogs smoking cigars and playing poker. This is one particular scene often hard to find that will sell very quickly. You don't have to watch specifically for dogs playing poker, it can be cats mowing the lawn or cooking dinner, simply 'pretending' that they are humans.

6. Speaking of pictures and photos, if you come across any spooky, scary paintings in a thrift store, especially if they depict a doll, a child or a clown in a distorted way, they will sell really well. The older and more haunting the painting the higher its value and the more it will sell for. There are a lot of people out there searching for this kind of creepy stuff so while it may be frightening to have to keep it in your home while waiting for it to sell

it's worth it because someone somewhere will pay a lot of money to have it in their collection.

7. Scary masks will also sell very well. They can be Halloween, masquerade or a just an old weird mask of any variety. Just be sure to stay away from cheap masks that you can purchase at your local Walmart, as they are not highly sought after. Instead you want to look for well-made masks. They should look very real and be in good condition. And remember, the creepier that better!

And at the end of day when you are looking for items that you want to sell quickly, you need to look for things that you don't see on a regular basis as well as items that you cannot find at a local store or easily online. And if you ever come across any one of a kind items that means you've really scored! Many times these items will have been hand-made and highly unusual. Those are the items that no one else is going to be able to find!

Chapter 2
Super Strange Items That Bring in Big Money

The following items fall into their own category of "strange". Basically, they are rare items that you really need to keep a watch for while you are in thrift stores. These items tend to be quick sellers on eBay and Amazon as there's always people looking for them. So, although some of them may surprise you they can be a very good investment for your money. And something you can flip and make a profit from.

1. Kool-aid brand sneakers. This is an item that I would never have believed existed if I had not seen it for myself. But just thrift stores sell Adidas and Nike they also sell Kool-aid brand sneakers. Of course, if you are lucky enough to find these shoes you will need to act quickly as they are highly sought after and can be guaranteed to make a profit from.

2. Zombies are all the rage right now and believe it or not, even homemade zombie art can be sold. For example a recent sale was of a lamp that had been turned into zombie art. It had a doll attached to it and it was made to look very scary. This lamp sold for $30! Something like this can be pieced together for around $3 at most thrift stores. Even zombie like cemetery type memorabilia is creepy enough to entice buyers. All things "dead" and eerie will attract the zombie crowd.

3. Furniture made out of animal parts. This is one that may not seem so strange to some but when I say furniture made out of animal parts I mean lamps made

out of deer hooves or chandeliers made out of antlers. There are tons of items like this that you can find on a regular basis if you live in the right area. This is because those who do not live in these areas are willing to pay good money for such items. The same goes for stuffed animals. I don't mean stuffed toys, I am talking about taxidermy items. Like fish that have been mounted, deer heads and any other "stuffed" animals you come across. The only thing you need to check is the size, these can be hard to ship if they are large. You should also check to ensure that the hair is not falling out of the animal, this means it has not been cared for, or preserved properly, and no one is going to want to purchase it.

4. Ventriloquist dummies are something that you should always watch for! These do not have to be strange to sell, in fact if you find these dummies in good condition you will be able to find a buyer for them, but if you find strange looking ones, you will make even more money. As with any item you want to check the condition of the dummies and make sure that they are not falling apart and that they work properly, but ventriloquist dummies are a great find!

5. Junk drawer junk. Watch for items that you would usually find in your junk drawer at home such as old door bells, old remote controllers and such will sell quickly and these items are very easy to ship. Look for small items that people can use on a daily basis, these are guaranteed to sell and you will be able to turn a quick profit.

6. Jewelry is an item that always sells well but you want to again look for items that you cannot find on a regular basis. Items that are unusual as well as rare. These items can be handmade or even wooden pendants from Africa sell very well. Also anything with a gothic theme tends to sell. The creepier and dark the better.

7. African masks are something that you should keep an eye out for. Many people like to hang these on their walls but on occasion they do get donated to thrift stores. When this happens you have a great opportunity to make some quick cash. You may need to clean these up when you buy them and oil the wood, but as long as they are in decent condition you can sell them fairly quickly.

One tip that I want to give you before I finish this chapter is that you need to be very careful when choosing what time you list your items. If for example you are listing at 1 am, your listing is going to be pushed very far down the list by the time anyone wakes up and starts looking for an item. Remember just because you are awake, does not mean that your customers are awake. If you are listing on eBay using the auction style format, always consider what time the auction will be closing as you want to keep as many people actively bidding when it closes.

Chapter 3
All Things Old and Off the Wall Treasures

Of course you can sell many old items for a profit but many people believe that the items you will be looking for are only well known items such as tube radios but that is not true at all. There is a much wider pool of items to buy from when considering selling to the vintage collector.

1. Old photographs always sell well but watch for old photographs that are a bit strange of creepy. Remember there are always those paranormal buffs out there who are looking for items like this. When you look for these photographs make sure that what you are getting is an actual photograph and not a reprint. Of course you can sell reprints, but at $4 each it is going to take a long time for you to make any type of income.

2. Speaking of paranormal buffs if you come across anything that has to do with the world of paranormal while you are out thrift shopping make sure to pick it up. This could be something as simple as an old Ouija board to something as rare as a dybbuk box. Anything will a spiritually dark look to it consider buying. The spookier the better. Many people also list a lot of haunted items but if you want to sell something like that you would have to have some sort of proof, or personal experience with the item being haunted, since there are so many fakes out there and you wouldn't want to mislead someone buying something that's not authentic.

3. Vintage medical instruments are an item that many people will overlook when they are considering which items to list but many of these items will sell very quickly. You need to watch for items that are in good condition as well as in their original box.

4. Clothing is an item that many people do not take the time to even look at when they are in a thrift store, but you should keep your eye out for unusual or rare clothing items. One unusual item that sold on eBay was a loom dress, it actually sold for over $2,000. Keep an eye out for one of a kind items that people have made, these are the items that go for the most money. And when looking at thrift store clothing remember to check the pockets! Even the ones inside the coats! You'd be surprised what people leave inside their pockets and forget to check when donating clothes to the thrift store. Many times the thrift store workers are too busy to check each and every pocket and so some tend to get overlooked! And all it takes it one pocket to hold a hidden treasure.

5. Vintage tools with wooden handles are great items to sell, but you don't want to list just one item at a time. You will want to keep your eye out for these items when you are shopping and then when you have collected several you can sell them as a lot. Just like the medical tools, there are plenty of people out there who collect these or restore them and are willing to pay a lot of money for such items.

6. Vintage 1980's Hypercolor t-shirts sell for good money on eBay. These are usual multi colored tye dye looking shirts. The special thing about these shirts that make them unique is when the shirt touches heat, it changes colors. These are very popular in the rave culture today. In good condition they usually bring in over $50.

7. Gag gifts are also very popular items and the vintage ones are even more popular. Of course the better the condition of the gag gift, the more money you will get for it. Even simple items such as itching powder and fake poop still bring in money! One item that I find very often is a gag gift called rattlesnake eggs. This item has been around for a long time and I remember playing with it when I was a kid, back then you could get these for about $1 each, today you can sell them online for $20 each and you can sell them all day long!

Keep in mind when you are looking for oddities to sell, you will need to think outside the box. You can actually train your eye to spot these weird kinds of items while you're shopping.

Don't think about what the average person would want because you are not selling items to the average person. It is really good if you can find a niche and work on it for a while before venturing out to other areas. For example gag gifts would be a great place to start or start with paranormal items. Choose a niche that you find interesting and then expand from there.

Chapter 4
Oddities and Wacky Items for Sale

Remember that there is someone out there that will buy anything you list, you just have to make sure they are able to find your listing. I have even seen items such as pine cones sell on eBay. The trick is not to overlook something in the thrift store too quickly. Try to expand your way of thinking and research everything you think is out of the ordinary!

1. Watch for anything with a skull design on it. There are numerous buyers in the rockabilly crowd or retro crowd who love to collect items with this design. This can be a shirt, dress or anything really! There are plenty of people who are looking for these items and you will not be able to keep these items on your virtual shelves.

2. How to books and self-improvement books are also an item that you can sometimes sell very quickly. The ones that sell the best are the older books. The Art of Feminism and books from the 50's is one of the genres people are really looking for. That is not to say you should not keep an eye out for other types like how to draw, paint, etc., as they tend to sell quickly as well. Do some research on what the current pop culture trends are and that can help you zero in on a target market.

   Also remember when you're shopping for books, especially old vintage books, to flip through it to see if anyone left anything between its pages. I once found a $100 bill someone had put between the pages of an old Bible! So, you knew know what people tuck away within those covers.

3. JNCO mens vintage 1990's jeans sell great on eBay! These jeans usually have a very wide leg opening at the bottom and a lot of dragon style embroidered artwork on them. They were very popular in the skateboard culture in the 1990's. As a general rule, the larger the size, the more money you can expect to bring in.

4. Vintage McDonalds toys are another item that many people collect. If it came in a Happy Meal at one point in time, then you can bet there is someone out there probably looking for it. You need to make sure that these toys are still wrapped otherwise the chances of selling them are extremely low. I have seen a set of 4 stickers that came in a McDonalds Happy Meal go for $25 just because it was in its original wrapping.

5. Woman's purses are something that can be found in abundance at thrift stores and they are worth taking the time to look at. Purses always sell like crazy online and if you can snag a few good ones here and there you will be able to make a pretty penny off of them. Of course you don't want the average Walmart brand purse, you want something that is rare, old but in great condition or a well-known name. Also, always check inside the purses for items left behind! Just like with old books, people tend to be too busy to check the purses they're giving away to the thrift store and the thrift store workers are sometimes too busy a well to stop and check each and every purse that goes out onto the thrift store floor. And don't forget the zipper compartments! I've found money stashed in the zippered parts of purses before.

6. Keys are something that I find a lot of at thrift stores, but you have to watch for specific keys. You don't want to just purchase a bunch if random keys and expect that

they will sell online. However, if you can find some antique skeleton design keys you will be able to turn a quick profit. Most of the time you will find these and they will look rusted but if you clean them up and treat them with some oil they will look as good as new and will sell fairly quickly.

7.   Military items are also an item that you can sell a ton of and you can sell them very quickly. If you live close to a military base you will be able to find a ton of items at thrift stores there for very cheap. If you can find a uniform with a few patches on it you are going to be able to pull off the patches and sell them alone or you can sell the entire uniform. A lot of time you can find very old uniforms which are very popular, but even if you find something that is not old it is going to sell quickly.

Remember when you are looking for items to sell, the older they are the faster they are going to sell. However that is not to say that newer items will not sell as well. If you come across items that are new, have tags on them or have never been taken out of their boxes, it is worth spending a few dollars on and listing them. If you are able to list an item for about 50 percent or less of what it would cost new, you will be able to sell it.

Chapter 5
Thinking Outside the Collectible Box

I have stated several times in this book that if you want to sell oddities you are going to have to think outside the box and look for items that most sellers would overlook. And one great way to sell several items quickly is to create what's called a "Lot". This is when you sell several items all at once together in one big "group". It is of course best to make sure they all are in the same niche but even if you list a lot of random oddities together in a group chances are someone is going to buy the whole "lot" just so they can get their hands on one specific item within the group.

1. Native American items are also very popular. From peace pipes to moccasins collectors are always looking for these items. You can also watch for dolls that are made to look like Native Americans, paintings, dream catchers and so on. I have always been lucky enough to find several dream catchers when I go out to thrift stores and I have found that even the smallest dream catchers sell very quickly.

2. Always keep your eyes open for the vintage 1980's game called Crossbows and Catapults. This game routinely sells complete for over $150. There were a lot of additional accessories available when the game was popular. Many time you can find the game and also find a lot of the additional accessories included! There are also other vintage games that can bring in high profit.

3. The original NES Nintendo video game system always sells well as you may know. However, be on the lookout for ROB. He was the optional robot that could be purchased with the original system in the 1980's. In complete condition he will typically sell for over $100.

4. Moving on to the subject of glass, there are a few different types of glass items that you should watch for. Cobalt blue glass is very popular right now and if you can find a set of anything made out of this glass you will be able to sell it for a large profit. Hand blown green glass is something that is very rare but you really should watch for. I have found items that I paid $10 for and sold them for over $100 but you need to make sure that the glass is green and not green with another color swirled in or clear with green in it. Pay close attention to the color of the glass. Remember to always check the "new" stock that is coming out from behind the thrift stores closed doors! Keep your eye out for the workers as they bring all the new items from the back of the store. Often times they bring new things out several times a day so it can be worth asking the manager what the best times are to come shopping for the store's "new stock".

5. Fossils are another item that many people overlook and often times these get thrown away when they are given to thrift stores, so you may actually have to ask them to hold on to these items for you. Fossils are worth a lot of money online. The fossil does not have to be something huge, it can be small bird bones fossilized or even a fish. Size does not matter here but the condition of the fossil will. Make sure you know if the fossil is real and what the fossil is of. If you find a replica of a fossil don't worry those sell well also.

6. Anything to do with sports always sells well online but you want to look for items that are rare. Cards that you don't see on a regular basis, magazines about odd sports, even books about sports that are very old and not easy to find can make you a quick profit.

7. Colored vinyl is another thing that I am always looking out for. These records are usually rare and sell for much more than a regular black vinyl record. Even if the colored vinyl is scratched, it can still be purchased and sold for good money as people like to use colored vinyl for different DIY record projects!

8. Postcards and stamps from around the world are another item that you might want to watch out for while you are looking for items to sell. It is wonderful if you can find postcards that have not been written on, but even if they have there are still collectors out there who will want them. We all know that there are people out there who are looking for stamps and the great thing about them is that they are super easy to ship. Just make sure that the stamps have not been used.

9. 80's cartoon lunch boxes can be found at almost any thrift store that you go to and they are very easy to sell online. You can also get quite a bit of money for these if they are in good condition. You have to make sure that you are not paying too much for them. Often times the workers in thrift stores will know what they have when it comes to items like this and will place them under glass instead of out with the other items. Keep your eyes open for lunch boxes that have not been spotted by the workers and get them for as little as possible. Don't forget that when you are purchasing a lot of items it is very easy to talk these workers down on their prices. Don't think that just because an item has a specific price on it that that is what you have to pay for it.

10. Vintage analog synthesizers! As a general rule of thumb, the more knobs the better on the synthesizer. Be careful not to just go out and buy every little Casio keyboard you find. Most often those will not sell very well. If you get lucky enough to come across a Moog or vintage Roland synthesizer in a thrift shop, you can turn a huge profit on it. Always check to see what condition it is in before purchasing.

11. Garbage Pail Kid original stickers from the 1980 are extremely collectible. The better the condition, the more money you can expect to bring in. Some of the cards in the first few series in the mid 1980's bring in big bucks. Many times you can find these in huge amounts jammed in baseball card style boxes.

If you can find an item that is vintage or antique and has at least some beauty to it, then chances are that you can sell it on eBay and Amazon for a profit. Even if the item is not quite beautiful, as long as it has character, you will find someone out there who is looking for that specific item. Never turn an item away just because you wouldn't have it in your own home.

Chapter 6
A Few More Oddities

You may be thinking that it will be difficult for you to find these items at your local thrift stores and although many of them are fairly rare, don't be discouraged! You can find these oddities and other unusual items like them at almost every thrift store that you go to. Chances are that you might have to dig a little to find them because the items may be buried, but trust me they are there to be found! And don't forget when you're shopping to take a quick drive around the back of the thrift store. There you can many times check the trash bins and also ask the thrift store workers if they have any items they'll be throwing away that hasn't make it to the trash yet. Sometimes you just might be surprised what thrift stores throw away and would be willing to give you for free!

1. Salt and Pepper shakers. A lot of people love to collect salt and pepper shakers and although this specific item may not be much of an oddity, you need to keep an eye out for rare, vintage salt and pepper shakers. I recently found one that was a bass jumping out of water, I had never seen a set like this before so I grabbed it for 50 cents, listed it for $20 and sold it within the hour. Salt and pepper shakers like this one that cater to a specific hobby will always sell well. Santa, Easter and other holiday shakers will not because they can be found everywhere.

2. Shadow boxes used to be very popular and many people have started collecting them again. If you can find one that contains little trinkets you will make even more of a profit off of them. I have seen these sell for over $25.

3. Vampires are all the rage right now so if you find anything vampire related you will be sure to make a quick profit. Even something as odd as a doll casket will bring in around $100 so watch for everything vampire!

4. Vintage Christmas items sell great! There is a huge market for vintage Christmas décor. Vintage Christmas ornaments can be bought cheap at thrift stores in the spring and summer and sold for big time money in November!

5. Old empty tobacco tins are an item that seems like it would be garbage but as odd as it may seem, there are those who collect these and are willing to pay a lot of money for these. They do not have to be in the best condition, but of course, like any other item, the better the condition more money you will make off of it. This is a good item for you to collect several of and create a lot to sell.

6. 'Haunted' dolls are really starting to become popular on eBay. The ones that sell are the ones that have the best "creepiest" story attached to it. It isn't so important that the story can be proven but that it's written by a seller who knows how to tell the story well. Now this does not mean you that you should lie and make up stories, but if something you come across has a great history behind it be sure to make it part of the "package" for the buyer!

Chapter 7

A Few More Things to Look Out For

I want to finish up this book by giving you a few more oddities that you can find at thrift stores and sell on Amazon and eBay for a profit. Remember that these are items that most people would not think to sell so chances are you are going to be able to find them in abundance at thrift stores. Most of these are also small so it makes it so much easier to ship than if you were selling fine china or other items that most people try to sell.

1. Chubacabra, mermaids, Bigfoot and all other strange and mythical creatures. You can actually find these items at thrift stores, of course they are going to be some artist's creations but they are great items for you to flip for a profit. Even items such as a cast of a Bigfoot's foot or a mermaid scale will bring in a profit. The reason for this is that people love the strange and unusual and they love to believe that these creatures exist which means that when they have an opportunity to have a piece of these, real or fake, they jump at the chance.

2. Ash trays are something that can always be found at thrift stores but did you know that there are people who are searching for unusual ash trays? You want to be looking for anything that has an unusual theme to it. Also loud designs generally sell great!

3. Canes are another item that a lot of people collect and the stranger the better. So always check the canes and umbrellas out when you are browsing through your favorite thrift store. Once again, try and grab anything

that looks off the wall and unusual. Those designs are what is going to be in demand.

4. Circus items are wonderful items to purchase at thrift stores and you can usually get them at a very low cost and make a huge profit off of them. Anything that has to do with circus freak shows will bring in close to $100 even if it is just a circus flier with the freak show advertised on it. Other circus items that sell very well are old posters and even old ticket stubs. And don't forget to keep your eyes peeled for scary clowns! The creepier looking the better. Those can be especially frightening and you'd be amazed at the large groups of creepy clown collectors there are.

5. The last item that I have for you is any medical book, picture, painting or poster that shows strange abnormalities. For example an old book that shows conjoined twins or one that discusses some of the early and rare medical treatments. Many of these items are extremely sought after because they are so rare and you can bring in a large amount of money with them. Even items that smaller such as a medical illustration from the 16th century can bring in a few hundred dollars!

Those are the oddities that I have for you. Remember that you really can sell anything to anyone. You need to focus on the description of the item, make sure you describe it well and make it sound interesting. Be honest, but remember with many of these historical and off the wall items, 90 percent of the sale is in the description.

Conclusion

I hope this book was able to help you to discover some oddities that you can look for at thrift stores and sell for a profit on eBay or Amazon.

The next step is to create a list of items that you want to look for on your next trip to the thrift stores and get out there. Find some great oddities to sell on eBay and Amazon. Remember not every oddity is listed in this book so if you find something interesting grab it and take a chance on it!

Finally, if you enjoyed this book, then I'd like to ask you for a favor, would you be kind enough to leave a review for this book on Amazon? It'd be greatly appreciated!

Turning Thrift Store Electronics And Gadgets Into Cash Magic

50 DIFFERENT ELECTRONICS AND GADGETS YOU CAN BUY CHEAP AT THRIFT STORES AND RESELL ON EBAY AND AMAZON FOR HUGE PROFIT

RICK RILEY

Introduction

This book contains proven steps and strategies on how to turn ordinary electronics and gadgets that you would find at places such as garage sales and thrift stores into profits using eBay and Amazon. Could you use a little extra income, but cannot figure out where to begin? Well, this book is for you!

Electronic treasures are often found at thrift stores and garage sales that people really want to purchase. They will often go to the internet to find such treasures. Why not be the person who could provide their treasure? By knowing how to turn electronics and gadgets into profit, you're not only helping yourself out financially, you are also helping out someone who has been searching for that item. Here's the chance to turn your old electronics and those you find elsewhere into extra cash in your pocket!

Chapter 1- Why Should I Use Amazon and eBay?

There are websites out there that offer you the ability to sell your items and make a profit. However, how do you know you're getting the type of service you're looking for? You hear about fraud being committed all the time on websites such as Craigslist, and your first instinct is to take a step back and avoid the internet altogether. However, if used correctly, the internet can be a great resource for buying and selling items. It all depends on where you choose to go.

When I first started selling on the internet, I was leery myself. After all, the horror stories make you want to think twice. However, after doing some research, I have found that using the top websites of Amazon and eBay are quite safe and can help me turn a decent profit.

However, you might have some serious doubts about selling your items online. What if the customer doesn't pay? What happens if you can't sell your item? Well, these websites have you covered on all aspects of the sale. They make sure that you sales are secure and that you get paid what the customer buys it for.

Secure Payment Methods

If you're concerned about disclosing personal information, then you don't have to worry too much because all eBay transactions are handled through PayPal. PayPal is reputable and has been used for years to complete online transactions. So, you have the security of knowing that they will be an efficient method to secure your funds.

Options on How You Want to Sell Your Items

Between the two websites, you can either sell your item outright or put it up in an auction format. This helps you to get the best price for your sale as possible. So, do a little research on your specific item online in order to determine which method would work better for you. You can have accounts on both sites, so don't be afraid to choose one over the other if you think that you can make more with a different sale format.

You also have the opportunity to put your asking price on your item. If the buyer likes how much you're selling it for, then they will buy it. So, when pricing items outright, make sure that you're pricing it fairly and not shorting yourself in the transaction. By looking at similar items, you can get a good idea of how to sell yours.

Less Fraud

Unfortunately, fraud can happen anywhere. However, it seems to happen less on these websites because of the security measures they have set into place. Since they act a middle man for selling goods, you will hardly ever deal with scams from buyers or other sellers concerning your item. This adds a sense of security to the overall experience.

For example, if a buyer wins the auction or buys your item, you don't have to ship it until you're sure you've gotten paid. This takes the risk out of a buyer who simple wants to make your life miserable. Also, both websites offer a great return policy to make sure that a buyer gets what they paid for.

By knowing the benefits of selling on eBay and Amazon, you will feel more confident in posting and selling your items. However, be aware that the websites have to make money, too. So, expect to see fees when selling your items and be prepared to price your items in order to cover the fees that you know will come after the sale!

Once you understand the pros and cons of selling online, you will realize that it is a secure and easy process if you use the right websites. Take some time and evaluate how you would like to sell your items and what type of website will make this possible for you. Remember, you want to make a profit out of your items, so be sure that the method you choose will get you that desired result.

Chapter 2- Best Selling Electronic Items on eBay and Amazon

Now that we have established the benefits to using the websites of Amazon and eBay, we can look at the electronics that will sell on these sites the best. If you're trying to make money selling your electronics, you want to know whether or not they are even worth selling online and whether or not they are in demand by the buying crowd. If your item is in high demand, chances are that you can get a better price for what you're selling. So, without further ado, I'm going to list some of the top selling electronics that top the charts on Amazon and eBay!

Gaming Consoles

Video gaming consoles are always a hot item to resell on the internet. Even if they are older systems, there is still a high demand for them and people who are willing to pay for them. Actually, vintage video gaming systems are collectable and in high demand, whether they are working or not. So, if you come past an old Nintendo in a thrift store, don't be afraid to pick it up and try to resell it. Odds are, you will make a nice profit!

Video Games

Video games for all systems, old or new seem to be a hot item to buy online. However, you need to know a little about the popularity of the game before purchasing it. Some video games just didn't get great ratings, so knowing this will help you to not buy something that won't earn you much of a profit. Games for vintage systems are great sellers as well. Be aware, however, that the games need to by playable and in decent condition in order to get any sort of profit from them online!

Vintage Electronics

If you remember them as a child, chances are that someone is looking for them today. People are constantly looking for electronics that were popular during their childhood. If you come across something like this during your forays in the thrift store, don't be afraid to pick it up if it is selling at a reasonable price. You never know, you might have picked up a treasure and not even know it.

Walkman Cassette Players

Speaking of vintage electronics, name brand Walkmans are in high demand on Amazon and eBay. These can sell for a great profit if they are in great shape and of the right model. If you come across any type of Walkman in a thrift store, pick it up. You might just be finding something that is in high demand that can make you a pretty chunk of change.

Old Telephones

You might laugh, but old corded and cordless telephones are great sellers online. Even though the world has been taken over by cellular phones, people still seek old telephones to add to their homes. With corded phones, the older the phone, the more popular it is. So, if you're looking at an antique rotary phone, it might just be worth it to pick it up and try to sell it!

Lamps and Lighting

Different types of lamps and lighting are nice to sell online. If you're in a thrift store, look for unique and different lighting that might catch a person's eye. People like to have unique elements in their homes, so finding something that suits their style will be a great seller.

Character lighting is another great seller. If you find lamps that feature cartoon or Disney characters, pick them up.

People like to purchase these for children's rooms, and the more unique the piece, the better price you can get for it.

Pinball Machines

Whether it's a table top machine or a full sized pinball machine, these are hot items for people to purchase online. They are also hard to find, so if you have the opportunity to buy one, it will be well worth your time and money to buy it and resell it.

Handheld Video Games

Handheld video games were a huge item for children in the 1990s. Today, they are collector's items and they sell very well on the internet. Take some time and look out for some of these old games and pick them up when you have the chance. They could be little gold mines waiting to happen.

On the other hand, handheld gaming consoles, such as the Nintendo Gameboy Classic, is also a top seller online. These are also difficult to come by, so finding one in any condition is a treasure.

IPod

IPods of all generations can make a nice chunk of change on eBay and Amazon. Even if the unit isn't functional, people will buy these for their parts. The classic IPods tend to get the most money because they carry a higher capacity for storing music. However, the IPod touch is up and coming. So, no matter how old the IPod, it is a good investment to purchase it. If the model is no longer made, it might be in higher demand than the ones that are still readily available in stores.

Used Cell Phones

Used cell phones, especially smartphones, are a great item to resell online. As the technology advances, people will go for the new and get rid of the old. However, these old phones are still quite usable and still have a lot of life left in them. People will go to the internet to find deals on cell phones, so take advantage of this crowd and snatch up functional used cell phones when you see them!

Cameras

Different types of cameras can be worth a ton of money. If you're not knowledgeable with cameras, you might be passing by a great deal on a professional quality camera that has lenses that might sell for a lot of money. Film cameras are now becoming an item of the past and people seek them wherever they can find them. Think about it. If you go to the store to purchase a camera, you will very rarely find film cameras on store shelves. Use this to your advantage and when you find one, pick it up and sell it online!

Computers

Refurbished computers are a hot item online. Buying a new computer is costly, so people will often seek out computers that have been previously used and restored. If you have experience with computers, you might even be able to tweak a computer with desired elements that someone would be willing to pay money for. When you come past a computer in a thrift store, take into account its age and its capability to be resold. Even vintage computers can be resold for profit, so don't discount a computer simply because it's outdated.

Televisions

If you come across old tube televisions, these are in high demand amongst collectors. Since they are no longer made, people have started to collect them and the prices for an old tube television have risen drastically. On the same score, new televisions that are way underpriced at a thrift store can also bring a good price when resold online. So, just because you encounter a television at thrift store, don't think that it is total trash. People do donate items that they simply have no use for.

Portable Audio

Just like Walkmans are selling for high prices online, other forms of portable audio will also get a good price. For example, old portable cd players are in high demand among collectors. You have to be careful with these though because many of them that are donated are no longer operational. You might still be able to sell it for parts, but for the most part, a dead portable cd player is virtually worthless.

Other portable audio that can be sold online for great prices include any type of MP3 player. Having the capability to take music and media on the go is huge among the general public. So, take some time and look through the smaller items in this section. You never know what you might find.

Tablets

Within the last couple of years, tablets have taken over the electronics world. People like these because they function as a miniature computer without the hassle of carrying around a laptop. The fact that they are extremely portable is their best selling point. There are many different brands of tablets that are being sold, so make sure that you know which brands are good and which ones have lower ratings. You might waste your money if you buy a tablet that nobody wants because of bad ratings.

Vintage Calculators

In the world of collectors, old calculators have great value. Many of these are the older model graphing calculators. Certain models will sell of more on the market than others, so if you're looking to buy a used graphing calculator, check out which models are in highest demand.

Electronics make peoples' lives easier. So, when they are good or if they have collectible value, they can often get a great price when resold. Remember, not every person is able to find what they are looking for electronics-wise, so you might just be offering them something that they have been desperately searching for! Just because it has no value to you doesn't mean that it doesn't have value to someone else.

Chapter 3- How to Find These Items Wherever You Are

Before I go to the thrift stores, I check out the top selling items on the websites that I hope to sell on. Most of the top websites, including Amazon and eBay have lists of items that have been selling more than others within a certain time period. Take note of the types of items that seem to be selling and keep an eye out for them when you are making your rounds to thrift stores.

Depending on the area you live in, you have different chances of finding some items than others. For example, you might find newer electronic items in areas where the population has a higher income. They have the money to be able to update their electronics more frequently than those who don't have a higher income. So, if you're looking for these types of electronics, go to thrift stores in the areas that cater to the higher income population.

You might give other thrift stores a chance and see what you can find. People donate items that you might not expect them to donate. Don't discount a thrift store based upon the surrounding demographics. Give even the most remote thrift stores a chance.

Tips for Finding Good Electronics in Thrift Stores

If you're leery of finding decent electronics in a thrift store, you're not alone. Many electronic items that are donated are often broken or unusable. This makes it difficult to resell them. How do you make sure that you're getting an item that can be resold for a decent price? Well, let's take a look at some ways that you can know if you're getting ripped off or getting a deal.

Testing Stations

In the past few years, I have noticed that a lot of the thrift stores have an area where you can test the electronic equipment so you know what you're buying before you actually purchase it. This can really work to your benefit because you can get idea if there are some small flaws with the equipment that can be looked past or if there is something that cannot be fixed whatsoever and you would be better leaving it behind. So, take advantage of the electronics testing stations in the thrift stores if they are offered.

Look at the Physical Condition

Sometimes the outward physical appearance of the electronic item can give you an idea of if there is something wrong with it working. If it's a highly sellable item, test it if possible. Often if the item has major external damage, it is damaged within. However, it can still have internal faults and still look okay on the outside. Use your judgement if you have doubts about the item.

If the Price is Right, Buy it

Even if the item appears to be damaged, if it is being sold for a relatively inexpensive amount, don't hesitate to purchase it.

The worst that can happen is that you cannot resell it. If it's a big item, make sure you do your inspection thoroughly before buying it. The item might seem overpriced, so wait it out if you feel that it would resell for a higher price. Thrift stores always have sales!

By knowing what you're buying and its condition, you stand a better chance at getting the most money out of it when it's resold. Finding the items can be the most difficult of the operation, so once you get past that, you are ready to go online and sell. Happy shopping!

Chapter 4- Gadgets that Sell Well on eBay and Amazon

High end electronics are not the only items that can sell on eBay and Amazon. Smaller electronics and gadgets can also resell for some good profits. These items are often easier to find in thrift stores and won't cost as much as the higher end electronics. However, just like the other electronic items, you must be careful about their condition and pricing. Here are some of the small electronics and gadgets that can be sold for good profits on the internet.

Wireless Routers

Any type of wireless router can be resold for a profit. Since buying a router new is expensive, people often turn to eBay and Amazon for better prices. Knowing this, when you find an operational router at a thrift store, know that someone out there is looking for a deal on one and might not think to go thrift shopping themselves.

GPS Systems

GPS systems are becoming increasingly popular since people tend to go more places and need directions. Finding a good GPS can be hard, but if you find one in a thrift store, you can easily resell it at a bargain to someone looking for that device!

Go Pros

Fitness is taking on new levels with the new devices out there to record and monitor your activity levels. Go Pros have become very popular because they are hands free and can take amazing video while the person is performing the task. Since these devices are rather pricey, if someone can find a deal on them online, they will buy them.

DVD and Blue Ray Players

Used DVD and Blue Ray players are a hot item if they are of a good brand and in good condition. Anyone can go and buy a new DVD player for cheap, but a good name brand player in good condition is more than likely going to sell better when resold online.

Adapters for Apple Products

Since most Apple devices only come with the cord that hooks into your computer, wall chargers and car chargers for Apple devices are great items to resell online. Since Apple is such an exclusive brand, their adapters and chargers tend to be expensive when bought brand new.

Record Players

Records are popular among collectors, so it stands to reason that old record players would be popular as well. However, you need to make sure that they are in good operational order. If you do try and resell one with defects, make it known in the listing. Most people don't want to buy broken devices.

Digital Recorders

Digital recorders can be bought for a low price and resold for a higher price online. Students and others like to have these devices for recording lectures and not having to take massive amounts of notes.

MP3 Players

As mentioned before, IPods and other MP3 players are popular for reselling online, despite their condition. People will often buy broken MP3 players for the parts to fix another player. Depending on the brand and the storage capacity, these can be resold for a nice profit.

Car Electronics

Car speakers and radios sell well online if they are of a quality brand. You need to know which car electronics brands are top notch in order to make a good investment when you see them sold at thrift stores.

Accessories for Popular Electronics

Accessories for cell phones and other electronics sell very well online. The better the condition and the brand name, the better the price you can resell it for. This can include headphones and microphones as well as webcams and other accessories for computers.

Surveillance Equipment

With safety being a concern for many families, surveillance equipment has become a hot item to be bought online. From cameras to keypads to set alarms in homes, people want to feel safe and are looking for the equipment to do so.

Cable Alternative Devices

In the past year or so, Amazon and other online companies have come up with ways to get premium programming without going through a cable company. A lot of these are in the form of a stick that will plug into your television and work with your internet connection.

Headphones

High end headphones will sell well online because it is less expensive to purchase them online rather than buying them new. Make yourself familiar with the top brands and look for them when shopping.

DVDs and Blue Ray Discs

With the prices of new discs rising in stores, people will seek out their movies on used discs. Depending upon the movie, its rarity and popularity, you can actually make a good profit by reselling these online. Thrift stores price them all the same, so they really don't take into account the titles or the condition of the discs.

Power Tools

Name brand power tools can be easily bought and resold if in good condition. Know what the top selling brands are and what models sell the best. When people buy used power tools, they look for the newer models, so if it looks older, it's probably not going to sell well.

Printers

Top brand printers and printer accessories are good to resell online. However, you must make sure that they are in good working order. People tend to look for top selling brands, so be aware of this when looking at these. The lower level brands can be bought new at cheap prices, so many people will buy them new. Don't waste your money on a cheap printer that you won't be able to resell.

Photo Printers

People like to print their own photos from the comfort of their home, so photo printers have become increasingly popular. These too can be pricey if purchased new, so people look for good quality used ones online.

Computer Software

Used and new computer software can be sold online as long as they are not outdated and the discs are in good condition. You also want to be aware that you're looking for the more popular software and not the stuff that no one has heard of before.

Vacuum Cleaners

Top name vacuum cleaners are also a great seller online as they are very expensive if bought at a retailer. Look for the top brands and make sure that they operate well before reselling them.

Kitchen Appliances

Small kitchen appliances such as blenders, microwaves, toaster ovens, and food processors are in high demand and people will search for and buy them online.

Small gadgets and electronics can be great sellers if they are priced right for the buyer and are in decent condition. People often turn to eBay and Amazon because they can find what they are looking for at a reduced price. Even if the item is used, they are still getting a bargain and are happy not to have to pay full price for the item. Keep this in mind while shopping for items to resell online. Think like a buyer would and you will find that you're buying items that can easily be resold.

Chapter 5- Knowing How to Price Your Items

Once you have your items, you might wonder how you can price them so that you are making money and the buyer is going to purchase it. This takes a little research and knowledge on your part. Not every item is going to sell for the same price. Since you are buying these items at a thrift store, they are more than likely going to be used and have a various array of defects. You have to take this into account when you price your item online or start the bidding for the item on eBay.

Look at Similar Items

Go onto the internet and look at what your item is selling for on eBay and Amazon. Both of these websites list the popular items and how much they sold for within the last day or so. You want to keep your pricing within the same range as similar items. If it is overpriced, you stand the chance of not being able to sell it and if you price it to cheap, you won't make much, if any, profit off of it.

Evaluate the Condition of Your Item

Since you are reselling a used item, you must take into account the damage and flaws that the item might have. These can range from scratches to small operating malfunctions. Depending on how good of shape the item is in, you can price it accordingly. People aren't going to buy something knowing that it has damages if they can get the same thing without the damage.

What did You Pay for it?

Keep in mind how much you paid for the item. You are trying to make a profit, so you don't want to lose money in the resale process. Price your items and start the auctions off to ensure that you are making money from your resale and not losing money or wasting time because you broke even. This might happen a few times, but being aware of the items original sale price will make it easier for you to price it to make a profit.

Allow for Shipping Costs

When you price your item, you have to take into account the shipping costs. More than likely, the buyer will pay this, but you must set the rate that they will pay for it to be shipped.

Make sure that you're allowing for a shipping cost for foreign sales because you can end up losing money if a foreign buyer purchases your item and you quote them the domestic shipping price.

At first, pricing used items can seem a little overwhelming, but knowing the condition of the item and how much similar items have sold for recently will help you to make a reasonable price for your item. By taking time to do a little research on the specific item and knowing what a fair price is for it, you will be better prepared to price it so that you make a profit and that it will sell quickly.

Chapter 6- How to Buy These Items in Thrift Stores

Thrift store shopping can be sensory overload for those who haven't done much of it in the past. However, when you get the hang of the shopping, you can easily find items to resell without feeling overwhelmed. Taking a structured approach to your shopping will make it much easier for you to get in and out and find what you're looking for. In this chapter, I'm going to give you a few hints on how to shop in thrift stores and get them at a bargain so that you can make a larger profit when reselling them.

Seek Items with Sale Stickers

Most thrift stores will price their items using different colored stickers. On certain days of the week, these stickers are half off, making the item an even better deal. Know which color is on sale that day when you're in the store and try and find items with these tags if at all possible.

Use Coupons

Some thrift stores will issue percent off coupons when you make a donation to the charity that they support. By combining these coupons with the low prices that the store offers, you can save even more money on the items that you're looking at.

Know What You're Looking for

One way to keep yourself from being overwhelmed is to know what you're going to look for even before you enter the store. If it's going to be video games, then focus on finding video games to resell. Don't let the store distract you. If you see other electronics that would be good for resale, don't be afraid to look at them as well. By being able to go straight for the area that you're planning on looking in, you will save yourself time and stress. Also, by knowing the specific type of item you want to focus on will help you to narrow down your search even more.

However, if the store you're in doesn't have the type of item you're looking for, it doesn't hurt to browse the section and see if there are any other items that would be useful for resale. You don't have to have a wasted trip even though you didn't find exactly what you were looking for.

Shop during Sale Days

If you want to make a larger profit, then going to a thrift store during a large sale day is another option. You will be dealing with more people, but if you know what you're looking for, you won't feel stressed out by the extra bodies in the store. Thrift stores tend to put their entire inventory on sale at least once a month. By knowing when these sales are, you stand a good chance at getting your item at a great price.

Know Your Thrift Store

At first, you're not going to know the layout and the policies of the thrift stores that you're shopping in. After a while, you will be able to go straight to the area that sells what you're looking for and be able to look through the inventory quickly and efficiently. Since thrift stores stock what is donated, their inventory constantly changes, so frequent visits are to your benefit.

Knowing your thrift stores and how to shop them during sales is going to be a great way to maximize your profit-making potential. Many people don't know how to shop during sales and end up spending more than they would if they were focused on the tags and dates. If you shop more than one store, keep a calendar of the sale dates so that you make sure you hit them for an opportunity to make the best profit when you resell your items.

Chapter 7- The Secrets to Turning Your Finds into Profits

Even though it takes some time and effort to get your business started selling electronics on eBay and Amazon, it will be worth it once you get the hang of it and know what to expect. From actually buying the item to selling and shipping it can seem like a long and drawn out process, but once you have a routine, it will seem easy and efficient.

At first, you're not going to know what you're looking for and what to look for. It takes time and research in order to find items that you can make into profits. Another factor that might inhibit you from making the most out of your reselling is that you don't know how to sell them. Selling on the internet is based on description and pictures. You must have both of these in order to make your item stand out.

Once you get good at pricing and finding items to sell, you will be well on your way to making great profits online. Since pricing can be tricky, learning how to price your items so that you make the most money and are attracting customers can have a find balance. This will take time and skill to perfect. Sometimes you're going to take a loss, but the ultimate goal is to make more money than what you spent on the item.

The great thing about reselling thrift store items is that you don't invest large amounts of money to buy your merchandise. If it doesn't sell or it turns out to not be worth what you thought, you're not taking a huge financial loss. After some time, you will become an expert at finding resale items that will earn you the maximum profits. Don't be disappointed if you don't see the profits come in right away.

Last of all, know what your customer is looking for. By catering to the people, you will be successful when reselling your items. You can find out what is popular by looking at eBay and Amazon and knowing what people are buying. Take some time to know what to look for and what people ultimately will pay for.

Good luck and happy selling!

Conclusion

I hope this book was able to help you to know what to look for when buying thrift store electronics to resell on eBay and Amazon. Electronics can be a tricky area to find decent and profitable items for resale, so knowing what to look for will be a great advantage to making maximum profits.

The next step is to take the steps in this book and go into a thrift store and find electronics you can sell for a profit. Knowing what to look for and what a fair price is are the first steps in making a nice profit.

Finally, if you enjoyed this book, then I'd like to ask you for a favor, would you be kind enough to leave a review for this book on Amazon? It'd be greatly appreciated!

TURNING THRIFT STORE VINTAGE TOYS INTO STACKS OF CASH

50 VINTAGE AND COLLECTIBLE TOYS YOU CAN BUY CHEAP AT THRIFT STORES AND RESELL ON EBAY AND AMAZON FOR HUGE PROFIT

RICK RILEY

Introduction

This book contains proven steps and strategies on how to find vintage toys in your local thrift store that will sell for a good amount of cash when resold online. Most of us don't know what toys will be worth money when we walk past them in a thrift store. To us, they seem like some child's used toys that need to be loved. However, there are massive treasures to be found if you are willing to look past the surface.

Finding vintage toys in a thrift store can be a quick and easy way to make some extra money. Collectors are forever looking for old toys to add to their collections, and they are willing to pay mad money for them. Why not take advantage of this opportunity? In this book, I'm going to provide you with some of the vintage toys that you can find in a thrift store that collectors will pay top dollar for. Why not give it a try?

Chapter 1- Dolls and Other Girls' Toys

In the wonderful world of thrift store shopping, there is a wide array of choices for everyone to look for. Some are simply old toys that a parent forced the child to part with because they had outgrown it. Others came from attics where they had sat for years, waiting for children to come and play with them. However their lives had started, they had all ended up in one common place: your local thrift store.

While some people don't think twice about getting rid of used toys and games, others have a sentimental link to them that makes it difficult for them to part with them. People may have had such a toy in their past that they would like to find once more. A lot of toys are only made for a limited time, so it can be difficult to find the same toy five to ten years after you have parted ways with it. However, if they existed once, they will be found again.

Many people turn to the internet to find such toys. How do you know which toys are being sought out? You can either turn to the internet or take a look at the timeless vintage toys that always seem to be in style. In this chapter, I'm going to list some of the girls' toys and dolls that make big money online.

Barbie Dolls

As time has gone on, Barbie dolls have become made of less expensive materials. So, if you can find the dolls that are mad out of heavy plastic, then you're looking at a collectable.

However, knowing your Barbies and the year that they were released will also help you to find rare and collectable dolls that people will pay good money for.

Old Plastic Dolls

Just like Barbie dolls, older dolls were made out of different materials. Heavy plastic, porcelain dolls, and those made of celluloid are all collectible and valuable for you to purchase. You can definitely tell an older doll by its materials and facial characteristics. They most often won't have moveable eyes or ones that are weighted. Also, they don't tend to be equipped to make much noise. There are older dolls that do boast these characteristics, but for the most part, they are plain and made of older materials.

Troll Dolls

Remember those crazy-haired dolls that promised good luck if you rubbed their tummies? Well, they are now a collector's items. Keep your eyes peeled for these goofy looking dolls while you scour your local thrift stores.

Old Tea Sets

Every little girl had a tea set. Well, now the older the tea set, the more valuable it is. Also, tea sets from overseas and made of porcelain are worth money. Also, be watchful of tea sets boasting characters from television shows or Disney movies. These are great ways to make a few extra bucks.

Kewpie Dolls

These adorable little dolls with the plastic curl on top of their heads have because a collector's item within the past ten years. You can find them in antique stores, but you might stand a good chance at finding some in thrift stores as well. The better condition that they're in, the more money they are worth.

Raggedy Ann and Andy Dolls

Again, these are common around antique stores, but they are also valuable when resold online. When looking through the toys, try to find authentic Raggedy Ann and Andy dolls in their original clothing. Collectors will pay top dollar for authentic dolls in good shape with original clothing.

Little Orphan Annie Toys and Outfits

Little Orphan Annie was a popular toy line in the early 1980s. Today, the dolls and the different accessories and clothing for the dolls are coveted by collectors. However, make sure that the clothing and dolls are authentic prior to purchasing them.

Rainbow Brite Dolls

Rainbow Brite and all of her friends were popular with the little girls in the 1980s. It's more difficult to find these dolls anymore, so if you see one, you know it will be a good investment!

Strawberry Shortcake Dolls

Strawberry Shortcake and the dolls that are a part of her clan are sought after by collectors. Be careful when buying these. You want to make sure that they are authentic and that the dolls themselves are in decent shape. Since collectors look at items that are in good shape, this is a good rule of thumb whenever you are looking at vintage toys.

Cabbage Patch Dolls

The original Cabbage Patch Dolls are one of the top items that people look for when searching for vintage dolls. The thing with the Cabbage Patch kid dolls, however, is that there was a knockoff of these that were sold in craft stores for crafting purposes. So, be aware of the characteristics of a real Cabbage Patch doll when observing these on a thrift store shelf.

While these are only a few of the toys that you might be able to resell for money on eBay, know that a lot of older toys to show wear and tear and other such damage. Take this into account when searching for toys. Some of these defects can be easily overcome, but others are beyond repair. I will cover what to look for in the way of damages in a later chapter.

Out of girls' toys, dolls are the most popular to be resold as a vintage toy. The other great thing about this is that thrift stores often have tons of dolls for you to look through. When looking through the selection, keep your eyes peeled for certain brands of dolls and the age of the dolls. These are both good indicators of whether or not they are considered vintage.

Chapter 2- Flashback to Your Childhood

It might make you feel old, but many of the toys that were popular during your childhood have come back with resounding popularity. Not only do collectors seek these out, but will also pay high prices to get their hands on some of these toys. With vintage toys, it's important that they are in good repair with as little damage as possible. If the buyer will have to restore it, then you will not get the highest price out of the sale. Keep this in mind as you're looking for vintage toys in your local thrift store. Even if you're not too old, toys from your childhood might still be considered vintage. It all depends on when they were made and their popularity when they were originally sold. In this chapter, I'm going to list some of the vintage toys that might just make you flashback to your own childhood!

Vintage Teenage Mutant Ninja Turtle Figurines

With the recent comeback of the children's cartoon, Teenage Mutant Ninja Turtles, the old figurines and toys associated with the original series are in high demand amongst toy enthusiasts and collectors. The toy line came out with many different toys and figurines during the original show's popularity in the early 1990s. So, look for these older toys when looking through thrift store shelves.

Beanie Babies

The original Beanie Babies have been a highly collectable item for some time now. Beanie Babies will have tags on them stating the animal's name and birthdate. People like to find Beanie Babies that have birthdates that coincide with their own. You might have heard some rumors about the original toys. They still have a high popularity rate, even with the viral internet scare of them being stuffed with spiders' eggs. Don't worry, they are perfectly safe, and people who collect them are looking for specific ones to complete their collection.

Pogs

The game of Pogs was played amongst preteens and teens during the 1990s. The challenge of turning these cardboard circles over with a metal disc happened to appeal to children. They were often found in abundance, but now they are a collectable item. So, if you should come across the cardboards circles and metal discs, know that they can be resold for cash!

Trading Card Games

There are a lot of trading card games that were popular throughout the 1990s that are still popular today. These card games have come out with different series based upon the year. The older cards that are not being made anymore, or those that are rare, are worth money to collectors. Look for card games such as Pokémon, Magic, My Little Pony, and Yu Gi Oh. These stand the highest chance of having collectable and coveted cards!

Lincoln Logs

These connectable logs were used to build houses and other such structures. They consisted of log looking pieces that had grooves at the ends, making them stackable. When put together, they had the feel of a log cabin. Since these are not made the way they used to be made, the original Lincoln Logs are worth some money when resold online.

Old Legos

Legos are a type of toy that is still highly popular today. However, when they first came out, they weren't as complex and specialized as they are today. The original Legos came in smaller sets and gradually evolved into the huge sets we see today. If you can find a complete set of old Legos, you can stand the chance of making some major cash when you resell them online.

Vintage Stuffed Animals

Most people can tell when a stuffed animal is old. They tend to lack tags and other markers that they were mass made. Older stuffed animals are also made of different materials. So, when looking at stuffed animals, take into account the material that they are made of and whether or not they have tags. These are good indicators of whether or not they are vintage.

Cast Iron Toys

Since the new movement towards toy safety, toys are no longer made out of cast iron. The heavy material could hurt children if the toys are not played with appropriately. So, if you find toys made of cast iron, it's a good indicator that they are vintage. There are a wide array of cast iron toys that can be searched for, ranging from toy vehicles to doll house furniture.

Fisher Price Toys before 1975

Fisher Price, a company that is known for creating toys for young children, is a highly sought out brand when looking at vintage toys. The older toys from this company are collected by toy enthusiasts. A good indicator of whether they are considered vintage is when they were made. As a general rule, I like to place the toys before 1975 into the category of vintage.

Mr. Potato Head

Mr. Potato Head and his family have long been a favorite amongst children. Who else will let you change their facial appearances on a daily basis? The older models of these toys and their accessories are a popular purchase online. So, the next time you find yourself face to face with a Mr. Potato Head doll, think twice before passing him by!

Disney Character Items

Since the Disney cartoons have touched many generations, toys based upon the characters found in their movies and cartoons are highly coveted by collectors. The older the toys, the more that they will be worth. You can easily tell which of these toys are older based upon the details of the toy. The older Mickey Mouse characters have larger features. So, by knowing which of these toys are older, you stand a better chance at finding a vintage Disney toy.

If you see a toy that reminds you of your childhood, depending on your age, chances are that it is no longer made and that it can be worth some serious cash. Take some time and look through the selection of toys in your thrift store, and if you have any doubts about the age of the toy, pick it up. Go with your gut instinct. The worst that can happen is that you're out a few bucks and end up re-donating a toy!

Chapter 3- Boys' Toys and Other Fun

Just like toys that were made to cater to little girls, there is a large amount of toys that are for boys that are now worth money. The selection of these toys is a little more diverse for boys, so you stand a better chance at finding something vintage for a boy. However, a lot of toys were never gender specific, so they can fall into any category. In this chapter, I'm going cover the main toys that are high in popularity that were made for boys.

Soldier Figurines

If you think about little boys, one of the toys that are commonly associated with them are soldiers. Soldier dolls and figurines are highly collectable and popular. Depending on the type of material that they are made of, these can bring in varying amounts of cash.

Hot Wheels Cars

Hot Wheels cars, especially the ones that are no longer made, are sought out by collectors. In their time, Hot Wheels have come out with many limited edition toys that collectors would love to get their hands on. While looking through toys, take note of the year that the car or truck was made. It's often printed on the bottom of the car with the Hot Wheels logo. Like other popular toys, Hot Wheels has a lot of knock offs that look similar, but are not worth anything.

Metal Dump Trucks

The old heavy metal dump trucks that little boys used to have are now a vintage toy item. The companies have stopped making these out of metal due to the dangers that sharp edges may cause children. Even though they have stopped making these toys, people will seek out the old metal dump trucks because they are durable and will last for a long time.

Star Wars Figurines and Accessories

Star Wars has been a long time favorite for many generations. With that being said, it stands to reason that the toys and figurines that come from the movie are collectible items. The older the item, the greater the possibility of it being worth some major cash. So, keep yourself on the lookout for Star Wars items!

Super Hero Toys and Accessories

The super heroes from the comic books have been a favorite to adults and children alike. From Superman to the Hulk, items that boast super hero logos and likenesses are popular and will sell for big money. I know that Batman and Superman were popular during my own childhood and are still popular with children today. Use the knowledge of super heroes to find items that you will be able to make a huge profit off of.

Ventriloquist Dolls

Ventriloquist dolls were an extremely popular toy among young boys in the sixties and seventies. The ability to have a doll that you could make talk was very appealing. Even though they are not popular with the children today, these dolls are still collected.

GI Joe Dolls and Accessories

GI Joe was a role model for young boys around the time of the Vietnam War. Having this fictional role model helped boys achieve creativity and bravery. The dolls and accessories remained popular for many years, and now the toys are being sold for nice profits.

Transformers

Based upon a cartoon, these vehicles that turn into action figures were a favorite among young boys. By moving their parts around, you could either have a vehicle or a person. These characters would fight the bad guys and win. The show no longer exists, but the toys can still be found and resold for stacks of cash.

Erector Sets

Erector sets were a project where a child could build structures using metal parts. This toy catered to older boys, and it was challenging and fun for them. They were only marketed for a short time, but people still seek to collect them.

Toys gain popularity for various reasons. By knowing what children enjoyed during the past, you will have a good idea of what will be collected now. Also, look at what's popular now. Trends tend to repeat themselves, so toys that were popular during your childhood may become popular once more. Take this into account when shopping in your local thrift store.

Chapter 4- Games and Puzzles

Every child likes games and puzzles. As they have evolved with time, the older versions of some games have faded into the past, while others remain strong up to this day. Depending on how rare and popular the games were, you can stand a chance at making a good profit by finding and reselling vintage games and puzzles. It might be difficult to figure out whether or not these items are considered vintage, but they tend to follow some of the same rules as the other toys in this book do.

In this chapter, I'm going to highlight some of the main toys and puzzles that are searched for and bought frequently online.

Old Wooden Blocks

The old fashioned wooden blocks that young children used to use to learn their letters and numbers are considered a vintage item that can be worth some money, depending on how old they are. When looking at wooden blocks that have the alphabet and numbers painted on them, take a look at the quality of the wood and that will help you determine the age of the block. The older blocks tend to be made out of high quality wood.

Pinball Machines

Whether it be a tabletop machine or a full pinball machine like you would find in an arcade, collectors are looking for these to add to their collections. Since arcades are becoming less popular, these machines have started to fade into the background, making them a good item to resell when found.

Table Hockey

Table hockey or air hockey tables are another type of collectible game that will resell very well online. As with pinball machines, since arcades are becoming less popular, these have faded out with time. Having a good and quality table will certainly earn you some nice cash.

Chess Sets

Chess is a highly popular game all over the world. With that said, there are multiple variations of chess sets. I have seen them range from cartoon characters to intricate figurines that grace an ornate board. Since there are so many variations of pieces, people will buy ones that suit their fancy. Older sets are collected as antiques and people will pay a good amount of money to buy a set that suits them.

Cribbage Boards

Cribbage is a classic game that involves moving your pieces around a small but intricate board. These boards have been in circulation for many years, so the older the board, the more money you can fetch when selling it online. A lot of cribbage boards are made out of wood, so follow the hints in looking at the quality of the wood. The pieces are often stored in a slot underneath the board, so if it has a metal door, you know it is of higher quality than those that are made with plastic.

Original Board Games

Vintage board games have a nice level of popularity online. Take Monopoly for example. The original game came out in the 1930s and several variations of the game have come along since then. Having an old Monopoly game can earn you a nice chunk of change if all of the pieces are present and the board is in good shape. There are other original board games that can be considered vintage, so think back to what games were popular during your childhood and see if you can resell them online if you should happen upon them in a thrift store.

Maj Jong Tiles

Nowadays, one can play Maj Jong on the computer. However, the game originated centuries ago, using brightly colored tiles that you set up and tried to match in order to complete the puzzle. These tiles are worth some good money if you can find a unique or intricate set.

Wooden Puzzles

You probably remember the heavy wooden puzzles that young children played with before they graduated to the more detailed puzzles. Some of these puzzles are very old and worth a lot of money. Depending on the condition of the puzzle and whether or not all of the pieces are present are also other factors that will determine the profitability of these when resold online.

Finding a game or puzzle that can be resold online basically depends on the factors of having all of the pieces of the game and the condition of the game itself. Knowing this, try and find games and puzzles that have all or most of their components. You will be better able to resell these online. If a game is missing pieces, then it is difficult to find them anywhere if the game is out of production. Think like a collector when looking at these items. This will help you determine if it is a worthwhile purchase or a waste of time and money.

Chapter 5- Other Toys that Can be Worth Money

After covering the basic categories of toys, I realized that there are still some toys that really don't fit into the other categories, but they still can be considered vintage toys and worth some money when resold. So, I thought that I would devote this chapter to these toys that don't really fit inside the definitions of the other categories. As mentioned before, this is not an extensive list, but it is a list of the most popular toys to be bought online.

Pull and Push Toys

Wooden pull and push toys that were popular for young children are a hot item to be resold online. These toys typically made motions while the child would pull it or push it along, making it seem as though the child were leading an animal on a leash. These might seem simple at face value, but they are considered vintage and collectors will pay good money for these toys in good condition. The best quality and most likely to resell are going to be the wooden toys that still work properly.

My Little Pony

My Little Pony dolls and trading cards fit into the category because they are not necessarily popular with little girls. Grown men have taken a fancy to the card game and collecting the dolls. By finding the toys and the cards, you are basically guaranteeing yourself a sell online. Be careful about fakes though. There are pony figurines that will closely resemble the My Little Pony horses, but they are not the originals. So, when you come across an older looking My Little Pony horse, don't discount it as some poor reject from a little girl's collection.

Pez Machines

Pez machines might not seem like a toy, but kids love to play with them. Another thing about Pez machines is that there are millions of different ones and new ones are becoming available regularly. Since when a new machine is released there is only limited availability, collectors are willing to pay more if they cannot find the toy in stores or anywhere else. The older Pez machines are also highly collectable because they are no longer in production and coming across them is rare.

Waterfuls

These water games made for hours of entertainment for young children. The point of the game was to use water pressure to accomplish tasks such as placing rings around poles and moving small balls around a watery game land. These were popular in the 1990s, and finding one in good condition will definitely interest an avid collector.

Cap Guns

Cap guns were a realistic version of a real gun that even made a similar sound. You would put in cartridges that would pop when you pulled the trigger on the gun. Boys and girls alike liked to play cops and robbers using these realistic guns.

Yo-yos

Yo-yos are another type of toy that has evolved over time. They started out as wooded discs on a rope that would return when thrown correctly. As time went on, the wood was replaced by plastic and other variations of materials. These are a great selling item if you can find the old wooden yo-yos or one of the older plastic yo-yos.

View Masters

View Masters were a toy where a child could put in a disc and view whatever the discs had printed on them. It was kind of like looking a picture's negative with a magnifying glass. When you would hit the trigger, the disc would turn and a new picture or scene would fill your line of vision. There were multiple types of discs that could be viewed in these toys, ranging from scenery to comic book characters.

If you have a feeling that a toy is vintage and that you could sell it, try it. The good thing about thrift stores is that they don't charge a lot of money for items. You will stand a better chance of making your money back plus a profit on most of the items you buy and resell. Don't be afraid to take a chance. It might be a better investment than you could have imagined!

Chapter 6- Knowing Whether or Not to Buy

When looking through the endless piles of toys at your local thrift store, you might be confused as to the quality and resale capabilities of the toy. For starters, how do you know if it's simply a thrown out piece of garbage, a knockoff, or a real collector's item? These are tough questions to answer, and it might take you time to figure out exactly what toys you can make some decent money on. In this chapter, I'm going to give you a few tips on what to look for before taking the leap and buying thrift store toys for reselling online.

Quality

As time has progressed, the quality of children's toys has become compromised. Toy companies are more concerned with the volume and their profits. Most toys are now mass produced, taking away from craftsmanship and quality. Take some time to look at the toys that you are considering buying. Are they made from quality materials? Do they seem like they were mass produced? Do they have trademarks or logos on them? By taking a closer look and determining the quality of the item, you stand a better chance at finding a high quality vintage item that can be resold for a good amount of money.

Age

A lot of vintage toys tend to look older. This doesn't mean that they are falling apart. It simply means that they have signs of being loved and used for some time. Along with looking at the quality of the toy's materials, look for signs that the toy has been around for some time. This can be signs such as chipped paint, scratches, or fading. Be careful if the toy is showing signs of damage. The age of the toy can often indicate if it is vintage or not.

Brands

A lot of vintage toys have brands associated with them. Toy brands such as Marx, Playskool, Fisher Price, and other major toy brands have been around for a long time and have a reputation for producing high quality toys. The Marx toys tend to be made of cast iron, making them heavy duty and durable. Playskool and Fisher Price boast a long reputation of making toddler toys that range from blocks to play sets.

Past Popularity

Toys that are based upon movies and cartoons tend to make a comeback if the show was popular during its original time. Take the Teenage Mutant Ninja Turtles for example. They were popular twenty-five years ago and are now coming back, making the original toys popular and collectible.

Look at the Internet

Before going to your thrift store, look on the internet to see what toys are selling well. Try and find those types of toys when shopping. If they are selling well, odds are that you can turn a profit from reselling them yourself. By taking the time to know what sells, you are saving yourself money by not purchasing toys that are not going to give you the maximum profit.

Authenticity

When a toy becomes popular, other companies will try to capitalize on this fact by making similar products. These are not the originals, and they do not hold the same monetary and sentimental value as the original would. By taking a close look at the toy, you will be able to determine whether this toy is one of the originals or one that is made to look like the original so that someone could make some extra money.

Condition of the Toy

The amount of profit that you are able to turn on a toy is highly dependent upon the condition that it is sold in. Since toys often get damaged and altered, make sure that you are taking into account whether or not the clothing and other features of the toy are original. You want to purchase a toy in as close to perfect condition as possible, so major flaws in the toy might be a reason to leave it behind.

When considering your thrift store toy purchase, make sure that you are taking into account the condition and popularity the toys had in the past. The best piece of advice that I can give you is to look closely for markings from the maker of the company that will hint to its originality and value. Also, do your research online before shopping so that you know what will sell and what can be left for someone else to purchase.

Chapter 7- Knowing What to Look for

With so many toys and so many knockoffs out there, it is important to be an informed buyer and seller. Not only will it help you to sell future items, but it will also help your credibility with the online purchasing crowd. The worst thing that you can do is to sell someone a fake when they were expecting the original. Make sure that you are giving the seller what they are expecting and not a toy that closely resembles the original.

Buying thrift store toys is a hit or miss venture. Since you are dealing with items that children have loved and used for who knows how long, you are encountering toys in various conditions. Looking at toys for signs of damage and past repair will be a good way to determine whether or not you can get top dollar for the toy if you were to resell it. If there is too much wrong with the toy, then it might be a good idea to pass it up. People will go for the ones that show the best condition, so if you know that what you're looking at is not in the best shape, then it's likely that you will have trouble selling it.

There is also the possibility of restoring items to their original condition. Depending on the extent of the use and damage of the item, this can either be an inexpensive fix or a costly venture. Remember, you want to make money, not spend it. So, if it looks like a toy is beyond restoration and repair, leave it behind. If the toy is extremely rare, you might still consider purchasing it because collectors will put the time and effort into restoring toys that are rare and worth money. You won't make as much money off the item if you sell it in a less than perfect condition, but it is still possible to make a profit on damaged items.

Another factor that you will want to look for is signs of alterations to the original toy. For example, if you notice that a doll's hair has been cut. The doll will have to be restored in order for it to be in top condition, and replacing a doll's hair can be time consuming and expensive. You know children. They have a sense of creativity that will often be displayed in their toys.

When shopping for vintage toys, the best thing you can do is to be educated on what to look for. This book is just the beginning of the possibilities of what you can find in thrift stores that can be sold for stacks of cash. Another fact about the online world is that it is constantly changing. Some of the toys in this book might be popular now and not be in a year or two. By taking time to research what will sell online will help you to make informed purchases that will benefit your pocket book.

Good luck in your venture into selling thrift store vintage toys online for a profit! I know many people how have succeeded in turning a decent income from this simple task. It only takes a little time to make money! Remember, there are people out there who are looking for the items that sit on your thrift store's shelf. Help you and them by giving them what they are looking for!

Conclusion

I hope this book was able to help you to identify the toys that you can find and resell online for great profits. Sometimes it is difficult to evaluate whether or not the toy in front of you is vintage and in demand. By knowing what will sell online, you have a good chance at finding toys that will give you stacks of cash.

The next step is to go to your local thrift store and see if you can find any of the toys listed in this book. A stack of cash might be staring back at you from the shelf!

Finally, if you enjoyed this book, then I'd like to ask you for a favor, would you be kind enough to leave a review for this book on Amazon? It'd be greatly appreciated!

RESELLER SECRETS
TO DOMINATING A THRIFT STORE
REVEALED

40 Creative Ways To Use All Of The Sections In A Thrift Store To Make Huge Money Selling On eBay And Amazon

RICK RILEY

Introduction

This book contains proven steps and strategies on how to use all of the sections of your thrift store in creative ways so that you can make a huge profit selling on eBay and Amazon.

This book is going to teach you how you can use your creativity paired with the items you can regularly find at thrift stores to turn a huge profit. Unlike other books, this book is not just about finding those special treasures, but how you can use literally any item that you find in a thrift store to make a profit.

You will be walked through the different sections of a thrift store and given in great detail ideas that you can use to make a profit. At the end of this book you are going to be given tips ensuring that you are able to turn a profit and ensuring that you only purchase items that you will be able to resell.

Chapter 1
How to Buy and Sell Clothing From a Thrift Store

Often times it can be difficult to make very much money off of clothing that you purchase at a thrift store, unless you are able to find high end clothing. Of course we know that we can flip this type of item for a profit, but what about all the other clothing you find? In this chapter we are going to go over some creative ways for you to flip thrift store clothing and make a profit from it on eBay or Amazon.

1. Many times you can find a lot of plain t-shirts at thrift stores for pennies, but most people are not looking for this type of item when they shop eBay or Amazon. You should not pass these up however. Instead think about buying all of the white, cream and grey t-shirts, dresses and pants you can find. Then, take one day out of the month and spend it tie-dying them. So many people love the tie-dye look but they either don't have time to do it themselves or they simply don't understand how it is done. You can sell these tie-dye shirts for about $5 each so spending a few hours a month tie-dying thrift store clothing can turn into big profits!

2. If you go to the thrift store on a day when they are having what is called a bag sale, you can get a lot of clothing for pennies! A bag sale is when a store will allow you to put as much as you can in a bag and they charge one flat rate, usually a dollar for the entire bag, instead of charging per piece. Of course you are going to end up with a bunch of non-brand name clothing that you will not be able to sell. So when you get home, go

through the clothing and start cutting them into small quilting squares. Once you have enough squares, you can make a simple quilt and sell it for up to $150!

3. Make your own designs by using thrift store clothing as a base. Often times you will see shirts or light sweaters at thrift stores and wonder why anyone would ever wear that. However, have you ever asked yourself what you could actually do with it? For example, you may think that no one wants to wear a striped sweater, but have you ever considered that it could be turned into a simple cardigan that people would love? Maybe add a few buttons and really make it pop. You can also advertise this merchandise as one of a kind.

4. Grab a bunch of sweaters at the end of winter when the stores are trying to clear out their winter clearance and make some sweater sleeve boot socks. Boot socks are all the rage right now and you can make $5 a pair easy if they are cute. Try to focus on sweaters that have lace around the wrist or another pretty design and you will not be able to keep these on the shelves!

5. You will also notice that when you are looking through thrift store clothing there are a ton of gorgeous jeans for girls and women but many of them may be worn in one spot or even have a tear. You can take these home and use lace to embellish these jeans making them look amazing. Again you can advertise these as one of a kind and make a huge profit. If you find jeans with holes in them, you can ask for a discount at thrift stores making your profit even larger!

6. Another thing you can do with old jeans is cut them off into shorts, add lace trim around the bottom of the shorts and sell them for $15-$20 each. You just need to make sure that the lace is not scratchy or too rough on the skin. You can usually find this type of lace at thrift stores in the arts and crafts section for a few dollars. We will get more into that later though.

7. Remember how I told you that you can find a ton of old t-shirts at thrift stores? One thing that I love to do is go to the men's section and look for the largest t-shirts I can find, add some elastic to the inside of the t-shirt where my waist is and I have a cute dress. You can get t-shirts for almost nothing at a thrift store and this is another good item to stock up on when your store has a bag sale. It only takes a few minutes to add the elastic. These dresses sell for about $20 each and if you want to get creative and add some more details, you can charge even more!

If you want to be able to make money off of anything you find in the clothing section of a thrift store then you are going to have to get creative. Most clothing items have been donated because the previous owners knew there was no real money to be made with them. Unless you are in a high end thrift store you are not going to find a ton of brand name clothing. Even then if you do go to a high end thrift store, there is not much profit to be made after you pay what they are charging. Instead, offer one of a kind creations you have made from thrift store finds!

Chapter 2
How to Make Money Buying Shoes at Thrift Stores

Another item you will find in abundance at thrift store is shoes. The problem is that these shoes are not always in the best condition and often times they are scuffed up or just look worn out. In this chapter we are going to go over creative things you can do with these old shoes so that you can sell them on eBay or Amazon for a profit.

1. This is one of my favorite things to do and it doesn't take very much time at all. I find several pair of old heels. It does not matter the color as long as the shoe is not broken down or falling apart. I do not pay attention to the way the shoe looks, only that the shoe is not flattened out or the heel is not falling off. Once I get these shoes home I will cover them with glue and then sprinkle a ton of glitter on them. This way I am creating my own glitter shoes. One thing I have learned is that it is very hard to find glitter shoes for women and for girls, so these sell very quickly if you do a good job applying the glitter!

2. Find an old pair of flats at a resale shop that are no longer in fashion, but in good condition. Then, you can add lace or other material to make them look like new again. The process of gluing lace or other material onto shoes is very simple and hard to mess up as long as you are paying attention to what you are doing. The good thing is that if you do mess up you are only out a dollar or two, and you have learned what not to do along the way.

3. Adding jewels to shoes is another great idea. Simple tennis shoes can be made to look amazing if you take a few minutes and add some jewels to the area above the toe. You can also add jewels around the rim of heels to make them look new. Be creative when you are adding jewels to shoes, but remember to not go overboard. If you are paying full price for jewels, you want to make sure you are counting that into the price of the shoe. If you can't make the price of your jewels back, you may end up going out of business very quickly.

4. If you find a lot of heels that you can purchase very cheaply, you can cover them with some painters tape, leaving the toe area uncovered and use some spray paint to spice them up. One great thing about this is often times I will find 30 or 40 of the same pair of shoes at a thrift store and I am able to make them all different, as well as unique, which causes my profits to raise.

5. You will never have a problem finding plain bland heals at a thrift store and if you can get them super cheap you can make a huge profit simply by creating a bow and adding it to the shoe. Some people like to add big bows behind the heel and others prefer them on top of the shoe. However, as long as it looks cute, you will make a profit doing this.

6. Grab a pair of white high heels and cover the back of them in pearls. You will want to ensure that you have about half an inch of space between your pearls, but this gives new life to an old heel. You can also place these around the opening of the shoe, or even just a few around the toe area. If it looks good to you someone else is going to fall in love with it and purchase it from you. Again make sure you add the price of the pearls into the overall cost of the heel so you know you are making a profit.

7. Don't forget about feathers. Ladies love feathers and you can add these to old high heeled shoes for just around a dollar. This will make the shoes look completely new, original and amazing. Then you can turn around and sell them for a huge profit.

Often times people don't want to get very creative when it comes to purchasing items at thrift stores and finding ways to make a profit from them. If it was as simple as going to a thrift shop, buying items and making a profit from them everyone would do it. Sometimes you need to think of flipping thrift store items the same way you would think about flipping a house. It may take a little work but if you can double or triple your money it is always worth it.

Chapter 3
How to Make Money With Home Décor From a Thrift Store

You can find so much home décor at thrift store, but often times it looks old and worn out. Before you use any of the tips I am going to give you in this chapter make sure that you cannot make more of a profit by selling that old home décor without doing anything to it. Many times I have picked up an item with the idea of repurposing it and have found out when I got home that it was worth much more in its current condition than if I repurposed it.

1. Picture frames are a great item for you to pick up. You need to look for frames that look old with a lot of detail.

    Don't worry about the picture inside of the frame. Simply look at the frame and if it is not chipped or broken, you can take it home. Remove the glass, as well as the picture, clean up the frame and paint it. This is one of the items you want to check the value of before painting it! People are always looking for large old picture frames. If you can find one with an old photo of a person in it, you can usually get even higher profits from it.

2. Look for old trinkets as well! Old keys, locks, or tags, anything that looks old and you can create a beautiful wind chime out of it. There are people who collect wind chimes and the more unique, the more value it has. If you simply collect these trinkets and create a one of a kind wind chime you will be making a huge profit.

3. Another item that you can find an abundance of is scrabble tiles. Many stores have bags and bags of these for a dollar each. Use these to create coasters simply by gluing them together, sell them for $8 for a set of four and watch them fly off your shelves!

4. It is difficult to find full china sets at a thrift store, but what you can find is random tea cups. These can be used to make candles in and sold for about $20 a piece. It is very simple to purchase the wax and wick to make the candle and if you glue the cup to the saucer (if you can find a matching set) you can charge even more.

5. One thing that I love to do is make a huge profit out of something that doesn't cost more than a dollar. One way to do this is to purchase plastic toys. For example a small dinosaur, drill two holes in his back and place one toothbrush in each of the holes and sell it for a toothbrush holder. Parents go crazy for this type of item, but make sure you are not drilling into a toy that you could sell as is. You have to be very careful with toys when it comes to thrift stores because often times you will find that something you think has little or no value is actually worth a lot of money.

6. Purchase an old plain lamp shade and cover it with buttons or gems. Lamp shades are very expensive, but you can find them at a thrift store for around $1-$2. Clean them up and make them look new again and you can earn a huge profit. Even adding a few jewels around the top of a plain white lamp shade will easily bring in $20.

7. Take an old vase that you find at a thrift store and cover it in pennies, trinkets, buttons or gems. Use whatever you can find the cheapest at a thrift store, but make sure it looks unique. Simply use a hot glue gun to attach these to the vase.

The more unique your item the faster it is going to sell and the more profit you are going to make on it. When it comes to being creative with your items to sell them for a profit on eBay you want to make sure they are unique, but you also want to make sure it is something that someone is actually going to want to purchase. Simply having an item that is unlike any other is not going to guarantee a profit. You need to ask yourself if you would give the item as a gift or if you would purchase the item yourself. If the answer is no chances are you will not make a profit.

Chapter 4
How to Make Money Selling Arts and Crafts Items From a Thrift Store

Most thrift stores have an arts and crafts section and this can be utilized to make a ton of money. In this chapter we are going to go over the many different ways you can make money by using the arts and crafts section in your thrift store.

One great thing about thrift stores is that you can purchase crafting supplies super cheap. You have a few options when it comes to these supplies. You can gather them and use them to create your own crafts which we will discuss plenty of ideas in this chapter. You can also create lots of these supplies and sell them quickly. If you want to make the most profit you will want to use these supplies yourself.

1. Yarn is in abundance at thrift stores and the great thing about this yarn is that it is high quality yarn. You will pay less than half of what you would normally pay for it and in your spare time while you are sitting in front of the television you can crochet a blanket and sell it for $50!

2. Hair bows for little girls are selling like crazy and these only take a few minutes to make. You can purchase the ribbon at a resale shop, spend five minutes making a bow and sell it for $5 with no problems.

3. A really great thing I like to purchase is baby dolls in the arts and craft section. These usually sell for about a quarter each and you can use the material, ribbons and such that you find in the craft section to really dress them up. Doll collectors go crazy for this stuff because it is one of a kind.

4. You can use a lot of the items you find in the arts in the crafts area to embellish other items such as shoes and sell them for even more. Remember the more you can save at a thrift store, the higher your profit will be, so that means taking advantage of all that the thrift store has to offer.

5. Use the fabric to wrap around old or cheap picture frames to make them look amazing. You can also create a peg board out of these fabric wrapped picture frames. You can also make a chalkboard out of them. Remember creativity counts here!

6. Fake flowers are something thrift stores never seem to run out of and you can use these in a variety of ways. For example, you can add a flower to your hair bows and charge a little more. You can make barrettes that are several different flowers in a short amount of time and sell them or add the flowers to head bands. You can also add these flowers to the picture frames and give them a bit of personality.

7. Use a picture frame and a few of the supplies from the arts and crafts section and create some amazing 3D art work to sell. You will find that this type of item is going to sell quickly, again because it will be unique to your store. Buyers cannot go looking for a cheaper price and this is what you want. Of course you want to have items in your store that cannot be found other places. You also want to make sure your customers can find items at your store that they can find nowhere else. So, use your imagination and start making money!

It will really depend on the different types of arts and craft supplies that your store carries, as well as the amount of work you are willing to put into a project. You do want to make sure that you are not putting more work into a project than you will be paid for. For example if it is going to take you 3 days to complete a project and the value is only going to be $30, that is not a project you should really concern yourself with.

Most of the tips in this book can be done in your spare time. It is understandable that you are not going to take your normal 40 hours each week that you normally spend on purchasing thrift store items and selling them to work on this type of thing. These items are either for your spare time or for when it is hard for you to find items to resell.

Sometimes thrift stores go through dry periods where they just don't have any treasures to be found. That is when you should start selling these items. I suggest that while you are able to find treasures at your thrift stores that you still work on a few projects in your spare time. That way if the time comes where you have found nothing to sell, you can fall back on these items and still continue to earn money.

Chapter 5
How to Buy Small Appliances at Thrift Stores and Make Money

It is a little more difficult for you to get creative with small appliances and electronics. However, I want to include this chapter because I want you to understand that you really can make money with every section in your thrift store!

1. Watch for items that sell well but are not often found at thrift stores. One example being that I can go into any local thrift store and find bread makers. I can also go on eBay, look up bread maker and find the same one listed for $13 ending in 3 hours and no one has bid on it. The same thing goes for a George Foreman grill. You can purchase these for almost nothing any day of the week from a thrift store, list them on eBay for $2 and you will not be able to sell it for much profit at all. So make sure you are looking for rare items.

2. Food processors are one of the top five small appliances selling on eBay right now. You have to be very careful when you are looking for one to flip, because you want to get a multi-purpose food processor. A normal food processor may sell at some point, but what people are looking for right now is a way to save counter space and save themselves from having to purchase two different appliances when they can find one to do the work. Watch for multi-purpose small appliances, these will bring you the highest profits.

3. Rice cookers are another one of those multi-purpose items that you can sell for a profit. Rice cookers not only cook rice but the high end rice cookers can be used

for stews, soups as well as a variety of other foods. This makes buyers willing to pay top dollar for them.

4. Anything vintage will sell as well, even small vintage appliances. You need to make sure that these have all of their cords and it is best if you can find them still in their original boxes with any books that came with them. It does not matter what the appliance is when it comes to vintage, as long as it is in good condition.

5. Meat grinders are another item that you will be able to purchase from a thrift store and make a huge profit from but you need to make sure all the pieces are included. If you have a customer who is expecting an entire meat grinder and even one piece is missing, you will end up having to refund the money and you will have one upset customer.

6. Finally you should keep your eye out for flour grinders. Many people have gotten into grinding their own flour. Some of these people have decided it was too much of a hassle and are selling or donating their grinders to thrift stores. You can pick these up for $15-$20 and sell them for a huge profit, often up to $200.

Those are all of the tips I am going to give you when it comes to selling small appliances that you find at thrift stores. One of the reasons for this is because you have to consider shipping when it comes to large heavy items and many people do not want to deal with that hassle. The other reason is that selling different small appliances is very easy, all you have to do is ensure it is a brand name, it is in good working condition, and is something that you cannot find every day at a thrift store.

When it comes to electronics the same rules apply. For smaller electronics such as CD players or Walkmans, you need to carry some batteries around with you as well as a tape and CD that you know works and a set of headphones. This way you can test the device and make sure they actually do work. Often times just because something says it works at a thrift store does not really mean it works.

Chapter 6
Other Items You Can Profit From in a Thrift Store

I want to give you a few more ideas that you can use to make a profit from thrift store items. These are items that really did not fit in the other sections of this book, but that I still feel they are very important. In the final chapter I will give you some tips that will help to ensure you make the most from your items.

1. Coffee cups are a great way to make money on eBay. These are often over looked but they can be bought cheap and sold for a huge profit. This is an item that you can purchase as is and make a huge profit. Look for Disney mugs, Smurfs or even Peanuts. The only thing you have to do to make money!

2. Another way to make a profit from coffee mugs is to grab some nail polish and a bowl of water. Put a few drops of different color nail polishes in the water and quickly dip your cup in the nail polish. Pull the cup out and you will have personally designed cups that you can sell for a profit. Plain colored coffee mugs sell for about a quarter a piece at a thrift store and you can sell them for $7-$12 each.

3. Grab those white coffee mugs and using some chalk board paint and create chalk board coffee mugs. Add a piece of chalk and you can sell these for $16-$20 each!

4. You can create your own throw pillows from the material that you purchase at a thrift shop. You can also purchase the ones that are already made, use an iron to

add a cute saying and people will go crazy over them. Remember there is always someone out there looking to purchase what you have to sell.

5. Curtains are a great way to make money from flipping thrift store items, but you will find that you will not really be able to sell the curtains you find as is. Most of the curtains you will find will be lace panels. You can take these panels and add some of the material you found at the thrift store and make beautiful unique curtains. Using this same idea you can make cute shower curtains that will sell quickly and for a huge profit!

6. Right after Christmas is a great time to stock up on Christmas decorations such as Christmas balls. You can use these items to make wreaths or other Christmas décor. If you have room to store these and are not looking for a quick turn around, you will see large profits in the following year.

7. Jewelry always sells great but right now you can sell handmade jewelry for a huge profit. There are tons of books out there telling you how to make the jewelry, but if you really want to put your thrift store finds to work, grab some books and make your own beads out of the pages of the books. It is a very simple process, and it only takes some book pages, glue and a straw. You can sell the beads on their own or make cute jewelry out of them.

8. Cell phone covers can be purchased for a few cents at thrift stores, add a few gems and you have a new unique cell phone cover. Make sure you know what type of cell phone the cover fits before listing it and don't copy someone else's creating, remember uniqueness counts in this area.

9. Cell phone chargers are another item that you can find in abundance at the thrift store and can usually get them for pennies as well. Remember you want to make them unique. I have seen jeweled cell phone chargers go for as much as $20. These are small and easy to ship and you don't have to worry about them breaking during shipment.

10. Bedding is a great item that you don't have to be creative with but often times gets over looked, especially childrens bedding. Again this will be Disney, Peanuts, The Smurfs and such. You want to look for vintage bedding that is in good condition. It is best if it comes in a complete set but simply selling the sheets without a blanket will earn you a great profit as well.

11. Use old watches that you find at thrift stores and place them on the face of a clock instead of numbers. So many people collect clocks and this one is sure to sell quickly. You don't have to worry about doing any wiring or electrical work, simply glue the watches to the face of an old clock you find at the thrift store.

12. Use old t-shirts to create a t-shirt necklace. You can create t-shirt necklaces or infinity scarfs out of any plain t-shirt and it doesn't have to be in good condition either. This is a great way to make $10 off of a bunch of t-shirts you paid 10 cents each for.

13. You can purchase Easter decorations after Easter and just like the you would do for the Christmas décor, make wreaths or other decorations out of it. Hold it until the following year and watch your profits soar. Again, this is only if you are not looking for immediate profits and have the space to store the items.

14. Stuffed animals are an item that you don't have to be very creative to sell. You have to have an open mind when it comes to looking for them in thrift stores. Watch for items such as Puff the Magic Dragon, the original Smurfs, Scooby and other 80's plush toys. Many people think that beanie babies will sell, but the truth is that you are going to make more of a profit on these simple stuffed animals than you ever will on beanie babies.

15. Cuff links are usually easy to find when you go to thrift stores and they are very cheap. You can use these to create many different kinds of jewelry including cute earrings. Not only can you make a profit on these but you can sell them very quickly.

16. Halloween costumes are a great find! If you can find small ones and turn them in to pet costumes you can sell them year round. People love to dress up their animals and pet costumes sell quickly, so if you are looking for a quick profit make sure you try this.

Chapter 7

A Few Final Tips on Selling

To finish up this book I want to give you a few extra tips to help ensure you pick up the best items and make the most profit possible.

One of the first things you need to do is make sure that when you are purchasing clothing you check them for any flaw. I discussed how you could embellish torn jeans, however you need to make sure the tear is in an area that will look good if it is embellished and that the hole is not too big.

When it comes to other pieces of clothing such as t-shirts, you want to make sure there are no flaws because you will not be able to resell it no matter how creative you are with the design.

You also need to do a smell test. If clothing has a bad, moldy or musty smell you do not want to purchase them. Sometimes you can get this smell out by washing the clothing in white vinegar, but I have found it is not worth the risk of losing money.

Know what your budget is! This is one of the most important things you can learn. Often times people get so caught up in purchasing items to resell that they forget that they need to focus on how much they are spending. I advise that if you are going to use these tips you do it with one item at a time, see how your item sells and then decide how much you are willing to invest. Always make sure you stick to that budget.

The next tip I have for you is that you should choose a niche. This means that if you want to sell glitter shoes and jeweled purses that you really need to stick to this type of item as much as possible.

Time versus money. Many of these projects are very simple, they can be done within a few minutes, but for some of them you will need to weigh the time it takes you to complete the project versus the money you are making. If the money is not worth your time, then you should not do that specific project.

Create a formula for your success. You need to have a plan. How much time you will spend in thrift stores each week, what type of items you are looking for, how much money you are willing to invest and how much time you are willing to invest in listing products.

Finally make sure that your descriptions are detailed. You don't want to make a description that is only a few words because that will not draw the buyer's attention. Make sure you give as much detail as possible.

Conclusion

I hope this book was able to help you to find creative ways to use all the areas of your thrift shops to make the most profit.

The next step is to choose one tip from this book, try it and see how quickly your item sells. If the item sells quickly, go ahead and invest a bit more time if not then move on to the next tip that interests you the most.

Finally, if you enjoyed this book, then I'd like to ask you for a favor, would you be kind enough to leave a review for this book on Amazon? It'd be greatly appreciated!

INSTAGRAM MARKETING SECRETS

Revealed

40 Creative Ways To Build Your Brand Quickly And Gain Loyal Followers In Your Niche Fast

RICK RILEY

Introduction

This book contains proven steps and strategies on how to use the popular social networking app, Instagram to spread awareness of your business and gain a following.

All methods of advertising have been done. From television to banner ads, the business world knows how to spread the word about services and products. However, have you thought of other ways in which you can promote yourself that aren't typical? In this book, I'm going to outline how Instagram can be used to creatively build your business. It's not the most popular method of advertising, but it will definitely be effective if it is used right!

Chapter 1- What is Instagram?

In this day and age, technology keeps on expanding and finding new and different ways to connect and help people. Now that we have smartphones, IPad, and other types of technology that will keep us continually connected to the world, a huge amount of people are on the internet every moment. Depending on where you are, a simple social media post could touch thousands of lives. Yes, technology can be scary at times, too. However, since it is the way that our world is going, we must feel comfortable using it and having it benefit us.

When I started my small business, I had trouble trying to figure out routes to advertising. Television and banner ads are often passed by and not even glanced at anymore. People know what to ignore. So, why would I want to waste my advertising budget on something that no one looks at anymore? This is when I began to consider other avenues of putting myself and business out there. One day, I was looking at my phone and saw the app for Instagram. Since I am able to use this app to post pictures on my social media pages and to other followers of the app, the idea sparked in my mind to use Instagram as a way to promote my business.

Some of you might not know or understand what Instagram is. Many people are not tech savvy, and this can affect a business. Since the world is moving towards technology, I encourage you to learn and use methods that will get your name and business out there. It might take some time and self-education, but knowing the new trends in technology can help you to become more successful in your business ventures.

Now that we have established the need for new types of advertising and why technology is a great way to promote yourself, I'm going to talk about how to promote yourself with Instagram. For those of you who don't know or understand what Instagram is, I'm going to give you some details which will help you to understand why it's a great way to promote your business.

What is Instagram and how is it Used?

Instagram is an application that can be used to take pictures and video. These pictures and videos can be posted on other social media sites, such as Facebook, Twitter, and Flickr. The photos and videos come out square, not the typical wide pictures that you are used to seeing on the computer. When filming a video, you can film for up to fifteen seconds.

The app was developed in 2010 and has steadily increased in popularity. Millions of users worldwide have the app on their smartphones and other devices. As the app developed, the developers encouraged users to use hashtags to connect with other users. This has been a widely popular way of getting pictures and videos to go viral. When something goes viral, millions of people will see it, making it a hit online. This is a great way to expose yourself to the world.

In the app itself, you use the camera on your device to take a picture or video. After the photo is taken, you have the opportunity to run it through filters to change the appearance of the picture or video. The app comes stocked with dozens of different filters, so you can alter the textures, colors, and shapes within the photo that seemed so normal just a moment ago.

After you have your photo ready to post to social media, you are able to add hashtags to the photo to describe what it is and what is going on within it. People who are looking at these hashtags will be able to view the content that you have just uploaded.

Instagram is used by millions of people, many being in their teens to early thirties. The ability to customize your personal photos has been a huge plus to having and using this app. It can be found in the Apple Store, Google Play, and the

Windows Phone Store. The app is free and can be easily downloaded and used instantly.

How is Instagram Used?

As mentioned above, people use Instagram to share their personal videos on social media. However, that is not the only use for the app. Businesses have taken to advertising with it, and others have tried to promote their causes by using it. If you have a message to get across, then Instagram can be a tool to help you do that.

When you get ready to post your picture or video, the hashtags will guide other users to your content. Depending on the quality and catchiness of your content, it can then be shared with their friends, and their friends can continue to share it. The impact of one picture can be exponential!

Now that we have a basic understanding of Instagram, let's take a look at some creative ways that you can draw the masses to your business or cause by using this popular and well-known app! It can't hurt!

Chapter 2- How Can Instagram Help You Develop Followers?

Having followers and customers is incredibly important when it comes to running a business or a cause. If you don't have that support, then your cause will fail. However, people struggle to get this initial following, making it difficult to stay in business. Knowing this, the first step to gaining popularity is to get yourself out there and promote your niche. It might not be an easy task to begin with, but once you have loyal followers, then you will start to see a following rise up behind it.

Instagram is a great way to gain followers. By using the features of the app, such as hashtags, you can easily send a picture or video out onto the worldwide web for millions of people to view. If you are on any form of social media, you will see posts from Instagram all the time. It's these photos and videos that can be shared and sent around the world by simply clicking a share button.

However, you need to get the hang of using this app before you can professionally use it to promote yourself. I encourage you to download it right now if you do not have it already. Take some fun pictures and videos and play with the filters on the app to see what you can do. This might give you some ideas on how you can advertise using this form of social media.

Once you know the app and its features, it's time to get serious and use it to advertise and promote. Think of ways you can capture the essence of your business or cause. This can happen in many ways. It can be through words, objects or actions. Whatever you feel will catch the feel for your business, use it in a picture or video.

Taking your pictures and videos and editing them, you might find some amazing elements that will be an even better tool to helping you gain followers. Use your time and imagination to make the pictures and videos work for you. Once you have a great post, take it to your social media page and post it with hashtags. Keep an eye on your post and see how far it can go!

You might want to try a few test runs with other topics in your life before actually putting your business out there. It will give you a good idea of how to use the app and what you can do differently to make sure that your post will get shared and spread all over. You might have to play with the app for a while in order to get the results that you want. However, having the experience and knowledge is just one great way to make your technology work for you.

After you are comfortable, you are able to register for Instagram for business. This is an area that caters to businesses and will help you to promote your business on social media. This takes a few minutes. You can create a business user name and put a tab on your social media page which will take people who visit it to your Instagram photos and videos. This is great way to get your personal friends to go to your business page and start building word of mouth.

The next part of your adventures into using Instagram to promote yourself is getting creative and getting posts out there that will bring people to you! Let's take a look at some creative ways to use Instagram for promoting yourself and your business.

Chapter 3- How Can You Build Your Brand by Using Instagram?

Your brand and your image is a very important element of having a successful business. People want to know that they are using a company or business that they know and trust. Trust takes time and effort to build. However, every business needs to begin somewhere, so the beginning is always the most difficult. In this chapter, I'm going to share some creative ways that you can promote your brand using Instagram.

First and foremost, you need to have a vision for your business and a mission statement. This is how your business sees the world and how it will work with the world in order to make it a better place. Consider this carefully as you begin to put together materials for your marketing. You don't want people to get the wrong impression of you or your business.

Have a Motto

Every good brand has a motto attached to it. These mottos will stick with the consumer when they think about going to that type of business or purchasing a certain brand. Brand mottos are something that could benefit any business. So, find a good motto for your business and make it catchy. Use it in all of your advertising materials. Before you know it, your motto will be associated with your business and it will spread.

Have a Logo

Having a logo is just as important as having a motto or slogan. Just like your slogan, your logo needs to be unique so that it stands out in the minds of the people who view it. You don't want to be too flashy though. That will only result in people thinking that you're trying to get the business and not care about the quality of your products or services. Make it stand out and let the logo sell your business.

Show Your Vision through Your Ads

Knowing what your vision is will be essential to your business. You want your customers and the public to know what you stand for. This vision needs to be in all of your advertising efforts. Knowing what you stand for is important to the people who will be your customers. There are many people who will refuse to shop or use businesses that have conflicting visions.

Not everyone is going to like your vision, but at least you're putting yourself out there to everyone and they can choose whether or not they will use your products or services. Try to convey this through your videos, pictures and hashtags.

Use Creative Hashtags to Gain Attention

As mentioned in the previous chapters, hashtags have a huge part in Instagram. People will find your business by these. Make sure when you attach hashtags to your photos or videos that they describe what your business or product is all about. Use common and uncommon terms when putting hashtags on your photos. The common terms will help draw people to that photo and the uncommon terms will give your pictures more exposure. The general terms will lead them to you and the specific ones will lead directly to your business!

Start Your Own Hashtag Competition

Instagram has the wonderful ability to hold your own hashtag competitions. Your customers will love the opportunities to compete to put hashtags on your photos. This involves your followers and makes them feel like they have a part in the business, even if it's only on the surface. Not only do they feel involved, it makes your business seem fun and exciting. Don't be afraid to use all of your resources in order to promote your business.

Use Fill in the Blank Posts

Another way to interact with your customers and followers is by giving them the opportunity to give their opinions on your posts. Try using the fill in the blank method on your posts. For example, you own a restaurant and have a new menu item that is coming out next month. You want to get feedback from your followers on what they would like for this new items. So, you go and post on Instagram using a sentence like, "if I could eat anything, I would eat _____." Have your followers fill in the blank. This will give you a good idea on what the public is looking for so that you can cater to the wants and likes of your customers.

Have Followers Caption Your Photos

Captioning photos is another way to involve your customers and followers. Try posting a random photo and have your followers caption it for you. This can be fun to see what the public will come up with when it comes to putting a title to your photos. You can also have competitions on what captions are the best and most creative for your pictures. The more interaction that you have with your followers, the more likely they are to continue to pay attention to you and your business.

Have People Share How They Use Your Product in Their Own Instagram Photos

Another great idea to build a following is to encourage your current followers to post pictures of themselves using your product or service. This will show others that it is a product that is worth using and that they should try it as well. Let's face it, people like to take pictures of themselves all the time, so why not use this to your advantage? Encourage posts of people using your business. You can even make a contest out of this! Be creative and allow your followers to be creative as well!

Your brand is what you stand for. Using Instagram will help you to build and spread this brand to the ends of the earth. However, you want to make sure that the brand that you portray is actually the brand that you would like to have associated with your and your business' name. A negative brand image can lead to ultimate failure, so really think through what you want your brand to portray before going to social media!

Chapter 4- Creative Ways to Use Instagram to Market Your Business

In the business world, marketing your goods and services is the way to get your name and your brand out there. From there, you can use the sources of word of mouth and reputation to help aid you in your marketing efforts. You might have numerous ways that you choose to advertise. Instagram might just be one of these types. However, you don't want to do something that has already been done. You want your posts and ads to be unique and stand out so that you can become known for it. In this chapter, I'm going to offer you some ideas on how to do just that. Being creative with your marketing can make a huge difference in your business' success.

Make Your Followers a Part of Your Business

People like to feel like they are a part of something. Whether it be simply naming a product or giving their opinions, people will take advantage of any opportunity they can find to have a piece in your business. Customers feel valued when they feel like you respect them enough to have a part in whatever you're doing. You can use Instagram to make your customers feel welcomed by encouraging comments and suggestions. Allow them to post to your page. Do whatever it takes to make your customers feel like they matter.

Be Involved with Your Followers

Having an interaction with those who follow you is a great way to show that you are involved in your business and care about what it does. When a follower comments on your photos or videos, take the time to respond to their comments. This shows that you're paying attention to them and allowing their voices to be heard. Nothing is more frustrating than feeling as though the business you are working with is operated by a bunch of robots. Be personal and people will appreciate it.

Creative Photography

Since Instagram is based upon altering videos and photos, make yours the most creative that you can in order to draw attention to them. When advertising using this method, make sure the picture relates to your brand or product. However, use elements within the photo that add an image of fun and creativity. People dislike when ads are boring and they cannot relate to them. Find the audience that you wish to target and use what interests them in order to draw them to you and your business.

Using Video to Create Small Commercials

Having a jingle that can be recorded and posted via Instagram is a great way to advertise. You might have a slogan or motto already, but having a catchy jingle that you can record in a fifteen second time frame and post will help people remember your brand and your business when they need it. Have some fun with this. Even though it's a short video, you can actually pack a lot of promotional punch in it!

Give Your Customers Ideas on what is to come

People love to be in the know. So, by giving them previews of upcoming promotions and products, you are playing with their interests and making sure that they are going to come back to see when the product or service actually comes out. This is a great way to get people to come back over and over again if what you are providing interests them!

Make Yourself Real to Your Followers

Even though most of the retail world is covered by faceless corporations, people still like to know that they are dealing with another person. Make yourself a real person to them. Let them know that they are in business with a real entity and not just an idea. This will make it seem as though they have someone who they can picture as the face of the business and that adds an element of comfort.

When posting on Instagram, post pictures of yourself, your family, and your life. Doing real things can make a huge difference in how your business is viewed. Let your public get to know you rather than getting to simply know your product or service. Be real to them!

Promote Old and New Side by Side

Even though your business needs to transition and offer new products or services, the old ones will probably still be around for some time. Just because you are putting out new items, don't forget to promote your older ones as well. Take pictures of the products and services working together. This will give your customers the image that the old isn't being left behind, but that more is added to the mix.

Be clever when you take your pictures and videos and edit them for posting. You want to create ideas in the heads of your customers that will stick and remain there for some time to come. The more creative that you are with your posts, the better the chances are that your followers will remember them randomly and come back to your businesses page or go to your business itself!

Having a creative business Instagram account can help boost your business' exposure. The unusual elements are what people will remember, and that can be a huge plus in bringing in new and old customers. However, remember to be yourself. People want to deal with a real person who can relate to them.

Chapter 5- How to Use Instagram to Further Your Business Base

If you have already started your business and have a small business base, you might want to gain new and different types of clientele. Widening who you sell to can help increase your following and your profits. In the past, businesses had relied on marketing to different areas and demographics to make this happen. However, with the advent of internet advertising, it is possible to reach any demographic simply by posting on social media. In this chapter, we are going to look at how using Instagram can build your business base and bring new customers to your business.

Partner with Other Businesses via Instagram

If you know of other businesses that would fit into your niche and would help benefit your business, reach out to them. Many large companies will promote themselves with another large company. Having a partnership in advertising is like a symbiotic relationship and both businesses can benefit from it in some way.

Take pictures of your products together. Take pictures of the owners doing things together. Let people know that you and this other business go hand in hand and that both of your products will be beneficial to them. Once you begin to partner and advertise with another business, you will begin to be viewed as one being with the other. However, you will still want to keep your individual elements alive so that your business is viewed as insufficient on its own!

Launch Products on Instagram

You can use Instagram not only to build excitement for the release of a new product, but you can also release that product live on Instagram. Take a video of the launch and post it so that everyone can see that the product is now ready to be purchased. This will add an element of excitement because people will feel as though they were right there the moment that the product became available. This might be toying a little with the consumer's emotions, but knowing what they like and making them feel special can earn massive amounts of business for your company.

Ask Leading Questions about Your Products and Services

Along with posting pictures and videos about your products and services, go to the general public for their feedback concerning them. By asking them how they feel and for their opinions, you will be getting their true thoughts and feeling concerning your business. These might not be the most positive of comments, but you can definitely use them to make changes and learn from them. Remember, you are there for the consumer, so knowing that some are dissatisfied for a good reason will give you an opportunity to correct the wrong before you have too many upset customers. The positive feedback will let you know what you are doing right, and that will let you know what you can continue to do that is effective and will gain loyal followers and customers.

Encourage People to Comment on Your Posts

Being an active and interactive social media business owner is a great way to bring in loyal customers and followers. Not only do they appreciate a quality product, but they will appreciate a company that is there for them. When you post on Instagram and other social media, make sure you encourage your followers to comment on your posts and give your ideas. This is another way to get true and honest feedback for your business so that you can make the necessary improvements in order to ensure long and lasting relationships with your customers.

Use the Comments to Build Your Customers' Experiences

The great thing about social media is that you can share and make your followers experiences go hand in hand. By taking the comments that they leave on your pictures and videos, you can turn around and use them for the greater good of your business. Don't be afraid to mention your customers in posts, as long as you are not insulting them. People love to know that you are giving them personal attention.

You can do this through hashtags or other comments. Using their Instagram user name will highlight them within your text and send them a notification that you have tagged them. This will bring them back to your posts to see what you have posted.

Involve Your Customers

Since everyone has an opinion, let them express it. Ask them for thoughts and ideas concerning your business or services. Once they share their opinions, you are able to use those to learn what needs to be changed and what can be kept as is. The customers are a great sounding board and will enable you to improve your products and services. It may also give you an idea for new products and services that can benefit both you and your customers.

By taking the time to reach out and use Instagram to get a feel for where your business needs to go, you can build a larger customer base, making it possible to keep old customers and build new relationships. The point of your business is to build that relationship and make it thrive. So, do your best to build new and keep the old. It will be beneficial to you in the long run!

Chapter 6- Other Creative Uses for Instagram for Your Business

Since many businesses struggle to get going and maintain profits, advertising is important. A lot of business owners fail to advertise properly, making it difficult to be successful. By using your resources, you can actually advertise for little to no money. So, if you think advertising is expensive, then look at the ways in which you can use social media to market for free! Here are a few more ideas on how to creatively market your business using Instagram.

Use both Traditional and Technological Methods Together

Let's face it. Some people will never take to the new technology. I still know people who use a land line corded phone. These people will never be good candidates for using the new technology. However, you don't want to set yourself back from gaining new clientele by not using the new technology. So, why not put both together? Try using traditional means of advertising and adding the technological elements to it.

For example, you can post a sign in your business that advertises a product. You can place a QR code on the sign that will allow a tech savvy customer to link to your Instagram page. This will help them follow your business as well as reach those who have no idea what a QR code really is. Allow the forms of technology to work together so that you can gain a wide spectrum of customers. Don't limit yourself to one form of customer by leaving out other elements of advertising.

Bring the Business to the Customer

The great part about the internet and the tools that it offers is that everything can be instantaneous. This includes posting on social media about the products and services that your business offers. If they know that you have it and that they can get it from you, they will more than likely turn to you for that product or service. People like to have the convenience of knowing what they need and where to get it without having to spend a ton of time finding it. By bringing the business to them, you are providing them with that convenience and gaining yourself a loyal customer.

Timing Your Posts for Maximum Exposure without being Annoying

There are people and businesses that are constantly posting. If you see too many posts from them, you tend to want to hide them. Don't be that business. Learn when to post and how much is just enough to ensure that you are getting your business' exposure but not shoving it down the throats of your followers. The goal of using Instagram and social media is to gain and continue a business relationship, not to turn the customers off to your business by being obnoxious and annoying. When I post on Instagram, I tend to limit myself to one to two posts a day. This reminds my customers and followers that I'm still here, but I'm also not being like a small child jumping in front of them.

Keep On Top of Instagram Trends

Just like technology, social media is constantly changing and finding new areas to highlight. Knowing what sells and what is trending will make it possible for you to place your business right in the middle of the trend. Since the trend is a popular element of the app, use it to your benefit. Think about past trends. Businesses and individuals went with the trend and gained exposure. Take some time to see what is trending and place yourself and your business right in the middle of it.

Keep Track of Your Results on Instagram

By looking at your personal page on Instagram, you will be told how well your posts and pictures are performing on social media. This will give you an idea of how many people viewed your post, how many people commented on it, and how many liked or disliked it. Look at these statistics so that you know how to target your audience in the next series of posts and updates.

If you realize that your business has a lot of negative feedback concerning a post or picture, then it might be a good idea to rectify the situation and learn that this is an area that you won't want to go again. Learn by your past posts and comments in order to cater to your consumers and build lasting relationships.

Even though the business world can be difficult to navigate, knowing that you can use social media and technology to further your exposure in the public will help you to gain advertising opportunities and get the message out about your business. Being creative with your advertising will gain interest towards your product or service. By using Instagram and social media to boost your exposure as a business, you can gain new customers and keep your existing customers in the loop about what is happening. These are all wonderful benefit, so why not use them to aid you?

Chapter 7- Keeping Up with Changing Technology

In today's world, technology is changing constantly. When you think that you have mastered one form of technology, something new will come to surprise you. Tech savvy people live for technology. Technology can reach the entire world from your home. However, you will still find those who cannot keep up with it, making it more difficult to find a happy medium between where to advertise your business and making sure that you reach as many potential customers as you possibly can.

While keeping up with what's trending and what will be coming in the future, you also have to think about the people who like the older technology and are not willing to use anything new. If you don't take the time to cater to them, you might be losing one customer base that could greatly influence your business. Finding balance in marketing is important. Don't leave your older or less tech savvy customers behind because you don't use other forms of marketing. The older forms of marketing are still very valid, so make sure that you are covering all the bases when it comes to marketing your business.

Since technology is changing, you should be changing as well. The old forms of taking payments, advertising and contacting customers has really changed in the last ten to fifteen years. Knowing what technology will help aid your business, you can insure that you are giving your customers what they need and expect while making the bookkeeping end easier on you.

One great thing about changing technology is that the word gets out quickly. From ads on television to banners on the internet, people know when the next new thing is coming. Top companies that specialize in technology will preview their new products months before they actually launch them. You just need to pay attention to how popular the new technology is before jumping in head first.

Being confident in how well a new piece of technology will operate in the public is essential when purchasing it and putting it into use within your business. The last thing that you would want to do is have a piece of technology that will not be used and will ultimately be a waste of time and money. You might feel like you're behind the times, but it's better to know that you will benefit from the technology before implementing it into your business.

Finally, make sure you have a good balance of old and new. You don't want to leave customers out of your business because they don't have the technology to keep up. Use traditional forms of technology to reach as many people as you possibly can. By covering all bases, you are sure to make your business more visible and more successful.

Conclusion

I hope this book was able to help you to find ideas on how to market your business or cause using Instagram. Since social media is a great way to gain exposure and promote yourself, you can use it to market your business and gain extra exposure.

The next step is to set up your own business Instagram profile and begin to find creative ways to post pictures and video that will gain and keep the attention of the consumer. By understanding the different forms of marketing, you will be able to keep in touch with all corners of the consumer world.

Finally, if you enjoyed this book, then I'd like to ask you for a favor, would you be kind enough to leave a review for this book on Amazon? It'd be greatly appreciated!

TURNING THRIFT STORE CLOTHING INTO CASH

How To Dominate Thrift Stores And Garage Sales To Make Huge Money Selling Clothing On ebay

RICK RILEY

Introduction

This book contains proven steps and strategies on how to find clothing items and thrift stores and garage sales that can be resold on eBay. You might not think that thrift store clothing is worth much, but people donate items that they don't think have much value. From dresses to pants, thrift stores have little treasures hidden in them around every corner. Why not learn how to find these items and market them to make you serious money?

Thrift stores and garage sales are prime resources to find items that can be resold at a profit. However, not many people know what to look for when looking through the endless racks of garments. What kinds of clothing are worth more money? What are you looking for when scanning through the seemingly endless racks of clothing? In this book, we're going to break down the methods that can be used to find the clothing that can earn you a nice profit when sold on eBay. Why not make some money out of items that are given away? Take this journey with me and we will explore the methods that can be used to find just the right items to make your wallet sing!

Chapter 1- Are Clothes from Thrift Stores and Garage Sales Really Valuable?

Have you ever wondered if there could be ways to make extra money from something as simple as a garage sale or a thrift store? When shopping at a thrift store or garage sale, have you ever found a unique and valuable find? If either of these questions is a "yes," then you're reading the right book! Even better, have you thought about selling *clothing* that is sold at garage sales and thrift stores? Not many people think of reselling clothing for a profit. After all, the clothing that is sold in thrift stores are considered second hand and thrown away. We are going to take a closer look at the thought of selling clothing purchased from thrift stores and garage sales to make a huge impact on your wallet!

When you walk into a thrift store, the sight of clothing automatically floods your senses. More than half a thrift store is teeming with clothing racks. On these racks, you have often found outfits that you can wear to work at a fraction of the cost of buying them new. No one knows where you get them. However, in order to find what would be useful to you, you had to endure possible long periods of going through each garment and inspecting it. No one wants clothing with stains or tears, right?

Have you ever thought about the fact that there are some clothes on those racks that can be resold? Just because they grace the thrift store racks doesn't mean that they aren't worth anything. That is a common misconception. People tend to view items in the thrift store and garage sales as thrown away and damaged. That simply isn't true in most cases. Think about the reasons that you donate your used clothing to a thrift store. Is it damaged? Most likely not.

When people donate to thrift stores or sell items at a garage sale, it's because they no longer have use for the item. I know that when I scan a closet full of clothing, I don't pay attention to the labels. I focus on whether or not I've worn that particular garment within the last six months and the likelihood of ever wearing it again. I'm sure that many others do the same.

What does that mean for you? Well, the clothing that people donate will end up on the sales racks in the thrift stores and on tables at garage sales. The people who price the clothing might not be fashion savvy and underprice the items or simply want to get the clutter out of their closets. Volunteers and workers at thrift stores often have no idea the treasures they might hold in their hands. When they price them, they look at the quality of the garment, not the label or designer. Once the clothes are put on the racks to be sold, they are fair game. However, not many people really know that they can buy and resell these items to make a profit.

Even though the sheer volume of clothing in a thrift store can be intimidating, if you know what to look for, then you'll be prepared to tackle the racks. Make sure that you take time to do this. Ideally, you want to hit the thrift stores on days when there are fewer shoppers so that you don't feel crowded or rushed. Even though sales look appealing, the opportunities to find what you're looking for are less when elbow to elbow with the person next to you. By taking time and having the reign of the clothing racks, you stand a better chance at finding something that can be resold for a good amount of money.

Think about the possibilities. If you could take the time and really look through the racks in a thrift store or at a garage sale, would you? Would you do it if you knew that you could make a huge profit on eBay? I was reading the news just the other day and saw a story that really highlights my point. The story highlighted how a woman purchased a sweater at a thrift store for three dollars and found out later that it was really worth a few hundred dollars. What a surprise!

What if you can have a similar experience? If you are knowledgeable about clothing and brands, then why not give it a try? It's a simple and exciting process to get involved in. However, this process takes time and persistence. Clothing won't find itself and it won't list itself or ship itself. You must be dedicated to the process and willing to keep going to thrift stores and garage sales. Are you ready to get started?

You too can find these articles around your local thrift store. Just because they grace the racks of a second hand store doesn't mean that they aren't valuable. Just think of the mine field awaiting your scrutinizing eye. Knowing that you can find items that you can resell for a huge profit will make thrift stores and garage sales seem like a candy store to you! I encourage you to look through this book and try some of the ideas that I propose and see if you can make tons of extra money by reselling thrift store items on eBay. What have you got to lose?

Chapter 2- What to Look for at Thrift Stores and Garage Sales

Where do we begin? If you're like most people, the thought of looking through the multiple racks of clothing might seem intimidating. I must admit that the first time I walked into a thrift store to look at clothing, I was completely overwhelmed. The whole store seemed to be covered with racks of clothing, and I was totally lost with the sheer volume of what lay before me. Where would I start and how in the world was I going to find what I was looking for? Since that moment in time, I have vowed that I would help others in the same situation.

By knowing what to look for, you will feel less intimidated by the sheer volume of clothing that thrift stores carry. Pick a place to start and begin to look for the characteristics outlined in this chapter to help you find what you're looking for.

Most people know what brands are the most luxurious and are really worth money. Ten to one is that you won't find any of these screaming out at you from the hanger. Even though you don't recognize the name on the label doesn't make it less valuable. So, what do you look for when looking through the racks of clothing?

Materials

Most clothing tends to be made of cotton or polyester, so when you see clothing that is made out of other types of fabrics, take a closer look at the item. Fact is that fabrics such as silk or leather are worth more to begin with than cotton. A silk blouse or leather jacket can easily be resold at a profit.

However, when looking at these items, you really need to look at the listing of materials on the label. The more of the rarer material is present, the more likely that the piece will be worth more when resold. Take a closer look at the clothing that have the rarer materials and see if they are of enough quality for resale.

Condition of the Garment

Even if you find a piece of clothing that you believe could be worth some money when resold, then you really need to look at the full piece. If there is damage to the material, it isn't going to be worth as much as a piece of clothing that is in near flawless condition. When people buy clothing, they want it to be of near new quality, not torn, stained, or stretched. Take some time and really inspect the garment. Odds are that if you wouldn't buy it due to its condition, others will be less likely to as well.

The Label

Believe it or not, the label on a piece of clothing can tell you a lot about it. If you look at simple, every day clothing, you might notice that the tags are rather plan and all look alike. A good way to tell a quality piece of clothing is by looking at the tag. Look for the brand, the coloring of the tag and the details provided on the tag. The more elaborate the tag is, the higher quality the item. You will be looking at the tag for other selling elements, but the first impression is often a good clue as well.

Brand Names

Even though the top brands may not be starting back at you from the racks, brands do tend to carry a great detail about quality. While you might not find Prada and Gucci, you might be able to find some other top brands that can be sold at a great profit. Which brands do you look for?

Well, if you are looking for womens clothing to resell, you always want to keep an eye out for Eileen Fisher, St. John and Citron Santa Monica. These brands are stylish and have great resale value. Fendi, Guess, and Yves St Laurent are also top brands that can fetch a pretty penny when resold on eBay. If you're in doubt, take out your handy smart phone and take a look at the brand and its popularity!

You always want to be on the lookout for mens hawaiian shirts. You should be looking for brands like Tommy Bahama, Jams World and Nat Nast among others. You always want to be looking for loud, vibrant designs when it comes to hawaiian shirts. Also, if you can find hawaiian shirt brands like Kahala and Tori Richard, they sell as well. However, you want to be purchasing those lower end hawaiian shirts at around the $2 range. Always remember, in general, the bigger the better! Do not pass up those XXL and XXXL size shirts thinking that no one is looking for those sizes. They will still sell and usually these big sizes will snatch a higher dollar value than the smaller ones! If you find a hawaiian shirt that catches your eye, make sure and do some research before making a decision. There are many vintage hawaiian shirts that you may come across that could be worth big money. However, they may take a quick bit of research to see if it sells. You don't want to leave a $100 vintage shirt behind because you were unsure if it sells!

Another thing you want to be looking for is athletic clothing. However, you are only going to be looking to buy this if it is still in good condition. Look for womens athletic brands such as Lululemon and Athleta. You can also sell Nike Fit Dry clothing for a good price on eBay, however, you are going to want to buy Nike in the $2-3 range. Look for cycling jerseys as well. These are tight fitting athletic looking jerseys. Usually they have 3 panel pockets on the back. Look for brands like Bianchi, Shimano and Primal Wear.

Always look for vintage mens skateboard and surf clothing. The vintage 1980's skateboard brands Vision Street Wear and Powell Peralta vintage clothing can fetch a pretty penny. These usually have very loud and vibrant designs. When it comes to vintage surfing brands, always pick up Lightning Bolt and vintage OP clothing.

Remember that every single thrift store that sells clothing has numerous profitable items inside. It is true that in this day and age many of the thrift stores are becoming more aware of the value of clothing items. It can be very frustrating seeing the price on some of the clothing items at the thrift store. However, they will always be overlooking some brands. The people pricing the clothing at the thrift store don't know everything. This is where you can take advantage and make some big time money! The more knowledge you acquire when it comes to what styles and brands sell, the more money you will be able to make every single time you step into the thrift store!

If you find a nice, high end clothing brand with a light blemish, do not move past it right away. Take a look at it and evaluate how bad the blemish is and if it is worth buying to sell as a long tail item. I can't tell you how many times I have bought a shirt with a tiny blemish and resold it for good money. However, when selling these items, remember to always describe and take clear pictures of the blemish. This will save you a lot of headaches when your customer receives the shirt.

Where the Clothing was Made

We all know that most of our clothes are made in the USA, Mexico or China. The cost to make and manufacture these clothes is less, making it possible for clothing companies to produce more product and make a better profit. However, have you seen clothes on the racks that are made in other countries? Look at your label closely. Garments made in European countries tend to be of higher quality and will sell for more. When you come across these items, take a closer look at them and research the brand on your smart phone. You might just have a great find in your hands!

Details on the Clothing

If you have a gut feeling that an item of clothing might be more valuable, don't be afraid to pull it off the rack and take a closer look at it. Some pieces tend to go unnoticed by the uninformed consumer. However, when looking at the piece of clothing, look at the details. Does the item have fancy buttons, embellishments, or any other marker that would signal to you that some time was taken in the production of it? Just because it might not sport a designer label doesn't meant that it isn't valuable.

Sizes

The harder to find sizes on a normal store's shelf are a great find when looking for items to resell. Top brands tend to make clothing for popular sizes because they sell better than items for people who are not typical sized. This includes plus sizes, extra-long pants, and other factors that are not considered typical. These items often sell for much more online than items that are made for the average person.

Vintage Items

The older and rarer the items are, the greater the likelihood that these items are going to sell better. Look for items of clothing that would have been worn in different decades. People are constantly looking for vintage items, so your find will more than likely bring a good resale price.

Let's summarize all of the information that we just took in here. When going to a garage sale or a thrift store, you want to take the time to really look at the items. The first thing you should examine is the material that the item is made from. If you feel that the piece is of finer quality, take a closer look at the tag. What is the content of materials in the piece? Where was the item manufactured? Does the tag look high quality? If you find that the item could be of value, take an even closer look at it. Is the material in good shape? Are there stains or tears? Would you buy it for your own use due to its condition?

Once you have taken a thorough look at all the characteristics of the garment in front of you, you will more than likely have a good idea of whether or not this piece can be resold for a profit. Knowing what to look for is the key to finding a great item to resell. Don't be afraid to take your time, look at the brand on your smartphone, and really examine your find before deciding to make your purchase!

Chapter 3- How to Prepare Your Finds for Resale

Once you have your selection of clothing that you wish to resell, it's time to prepare them for resale on your eBay seller's page. If you don't have a seller account with eBay, it's free and easy to enroll. Take some time to fill out all of the information and you'll be ready to list items. I will cover how to set up your account in the next chapter. When selling your clothing items on eBay, there are several factors that you need to take into account in order to fetch the price desired for them. In this chapter, I'm going to give you some tips on what to do to make your clothing items shine on the resale website!

Wash it

Even though the items have the telltale thrift store smell to them, you will want to wash the clothing as suggested on the label. When companies manufacture clothing, they will give you instructions on how to wash and dry your items to make sure it stays in impeccable condition. Take the time to wash and dry your finds as designated. It will take away the thrift store smell and make the item look fresh and new.

Display it for Sale

As you are well aware, clothing is typically shapeless unless it's worn. However, you probably don't want to model your thrift store clothes for the camera to show them off. First of all, they are not going to be your size. Since you have found items that could be considered rare, it is more than likely they are not going to fit you well enough to look flattering in a picture. Second of all, you're not going to be able to take your own pictures to ensure that they reflect the item the way you want to. So, why not invest in a mannequin? A simple bust of a mannequin can add the shape and show the details of the fabric just as well as using a live model.

People really like to see what the clothing is going to look like on a person. If you're just picturing it laying on a flat surface, you're not giving the buyer a good idea of what it's going to look like on someone. Remember, you want to sell your item for the maximum value. Make it look good enough that the buyer will want it!

Pictures

How you photograph the clothing is another way to make sure you get the price you desire for your find. When taking the pictures, make sure that you're photographing the item to make it look wonderful. This means having a good background, proper lighting, and a good exposure on your camera. No one wants to see your other junk lying in the background. Think about your pictures being I a product catalogue. How do store clothing catalogues picture their items? Try to duplicate these features in your listing photos.

Positioning of Clothing

Another factor to look for when taking your pictures is to make them look nice. This means pressing them, steaming them, and placing them on the mannequin so that it gives your buyer a better idea of what the item really looks like. Take pictures at multiple angles, giving the seeker all the details. Take a picture of the tag as well.

Providing a Detailed Description

Take the time to write a detailed description of the piece. Be sure to mention the fine qualities of the fabric, if there is any damage to the item, and any other information that would be pertinent to the buyer. Remember, buyers hate when they receive an item that isn't the way it was described to them! Be honest. Let them know that the item has been used. If you would want to know it yourself, tell the buyer!

Having an eye catching and descriptive product heading

Don't be afraid to make your listing stand out by giving it a catchy and bold title. You want to catch the browser's attention, so make your listings stand apart from all of the others on the site. This means labeling your items differently than all the others. While they have their clothing listed with generalized descriptions, add even more description for the browser that might just keep scrolling. Another good way to make your items stand out is by making your heading in all capital letters. This grabs the attention right away and keeps the browser from missing it.

Once you have a listing that meets your satisfaction, post the item to the site. Make sure that you're available to answer questions from prospective buyers. Keeping track of your listings is important so that you can get top dollar for the clothing that you're posting.

Still feeling intimidated? If you're unfamiliar with the eBay process, I'll go over how to set up an account and list items in the next chapter. The tips in this chapter are good no matter how much experience you have selling on eBay. Don't be afraid to make your items look great to the customer. The more they know, the better you will look as a seller!

Chapter 4- Setting up and Using an eBay Seller Account

If you don't have an eBay seller's account, don't worry! Just because you don't have an account at this moment doesn't mean that you can't create on and be on your way to making huge money reselling used clothing! It's easy and it will be beneficial to have even if you don't continue to sell clothing!

The first step to getting the account is by going to the website and signing up for it. Answer all of the questions to the best of your knowledge. eBay keeps your information private, so don't be afraid to list your address and phone number. In the years since I've had my account, I don't think that they have contacted me once via telephone. They tend to do most of their communication through email. When listing your email, make sure you put one that you don't mind seeing advertisements through. They want to make you a huge part of their business, and you are often buried with ads about what they offer.

Once you have all of your information inserted, take the time to look around the website at similar items to the ones you plan to sell. Take notice of how they're displayed, the pricing, and the seller reviews. You want to take the examples of the sellers who have the highest ratings. Whatever they're doing is working!

Look through your seller's dashboard and take in all of the features of the website. The dashboard gives you an idea of your past selling history, how much you have made in the last twelve months, and specials on listing fees and selling fees. Yes, eBay does charge fees for listing and selling your items. They are a business, after all. Be prepared to have these fees pulled out of your earnings. The website is very upfront and forward about their fees, so take some time to get familiar with their policies.

Enter your listings on the website. Put up your pictures, give the thorough description, and give the buyer a price. You need to decide how you want to list the item. eBay offers you the choice to sell it for a set price, or you can put your item on an auction setting. Many sellers find that selling their items in lots sells the clothing much better. This depends on whether or not you believe your item is better sold alone or with similar items.

Make sure that you're checking you seller's dashboard on a daily basis. This will give you a good idea of how your items are performing in the auction, if the buyers have any questions, and when you can expect payment from items that are already sold. By making it a regular habit and knowing what is going on in your seller's store, you will know whether or not there is room for change or if what you're doing is successful. Good communication and quick shipping once the items sell is a huge part in making your buyers happy.

Don't be afraid to look at the examples of other sellers on eBay. Look at what sells and how they sell. Know as much about eBay as possible so that you can get the maximum benefit from the sale. Selling on eBay is meant to be a rewarding and easy experience.

Chapter 5- Pricing and Selling Your Clothing

If something seems to be priced too high for you, what is your first reaction? I tend to pass by. I cannot see the sense in paying more than I have to for clothing, amongst other items. Most buyers are this way. The trick to selling your items for the top price is to make sure you have a fair starting price to begin with.

When you list your clothing on eBay, pick a fair starting price.

If the item is of good quality and you know it's valuable, start your auction price a little higher than the typical ninety-nine cents. Those who are looking at your item will know if they are fairly priced.

Take some time and see what your clothing would sell for when new. This is a good indicator of how much you can sell the item used. A lot of times, used items will sell for half the price of what you would pay when buying them new. Take this into account when you start your listing for bidding. I recommend that you start your item at about a third of what you would like to sell it for. This ensures that the item won't be outrageously priced in the end and that the bidders are more willing to take a stab at putting in bids.

Once an item gets to a certain price point, people will stop bidding. Ideally, this will be around the price that you were expecting from the clothing item to begin with. One bad thing about eBay is that sometimes the top bidder won't pay. This can be both discouraging and frustrating. Just keep in mind that there are alternatives to make sure you get your money.

Make sure that you are communicating with your buyer. Send them an invoice if they haven't paid right away and ask them to send payment prior to shipping the item. Don't be too quick to mail out the item before payment is received. The buyer may not pay, and then you're out your item and your payment. Once you receive payment, then make sure you ship your item.

If you find that the top bidder doesn't pay, there are multiple avenues you can take through eBay. If communication with the buyer themselves is ineffective, there is a way to file a dispute. This gives the buyer the opportunity to pay within a certain time period. If the time period elapses, then you are able to resell your item in another auction or offer it to the next highest bidder.

Remember, you're running a business. You don't want to lose money by listing your items at too low of a price, and you don't want to be stuck with the item because you listed it at too high of a price. The trick to running a successful eBay business is to make sure you're offering your items at a fair starting price and not taking away from your profits. It might take some time to get the idea of pricing, but once you do, you're well on your way to making great profits by using eBay!

Chapter 6- Shipping that Will Make Your Buyer Smile

It's got to be one of the most frustrating things in the world to order something online with great anticipation, only to have it delivered with something amiss. Sadly, this happens way too often. The item can arrive damaged, not as expected, or not at all. How do you deal with the unthinkable when you place your package in the mail?

Proper packaging and shipping accounts for a lot of your feedback on eBay. You want to have great feedback in order to draw new buyers to your items and make sure you sell them. People are not only interested in your items, but also in your reputation as a seller. If two similar items are offered and one seller had poor ratings, it's more likely that the buyer will go for the other item. You want to make sure that you're doing whatever you can to ensure your eBay business is a successful one.

In this chapter, we are going to look at ways to make the shipping process one that will be favorable for both you and your buyer. Just because you've sold your item doesn't mean that the sale stops there! Let's take some time and look at some ways to make your buyer happy!

Include a personalized note

If you don't have time to write your buyer a personalized note, that's okay. However, by adding a special touch to the order makes your buyer feel special and that they're buying from a real person. Even if you don't have time to write a new note to every buyer, have one that represents you and what you stand for. I put mine on a computer file that I can use to print several out and insert into the boxes. My customers love finding them and knowing that I took the extra time to address them as people.

Package the item properly

A lot of the damages that happen to items during shipping are due to the lack of proper packaging to begin with. When you package your item for shipping, plan for the worst. You have no idea what happens to your package from the time that you ship it until it lands into your buyers hands other than the tracking information provided on the USPS website.

Make sure that you're packaging your items so that they arrive in the condition you sold them in. Even if the outer box or envelope has dents and dings on it, what's inside is what the buyer really wants. This might mean that you use packing peanuts and bubble wrap. (Yes, even on an item of clothing!) Don't be naïve enough to think that a garment will not be affected by shipping too much because it's not breakable!

Price your shipping fairly

You should only be charging your buyer what it will cost you to ship your item. Many sellers use flat rate boxes. This is a good way to ensure that you're able to list your shipping rate for the buyer accurately and they know what to expect when checking out on the website. By using a flat rate box or envelope, you know beforehand how much it's going to cost to send it. When listing your item, know what size of box or envelope will be necessary to ship it without damage. This will help you to determine how much shipping is going to cost the buyer.

Offer insurance

When sending your package, purchase the extra insurance on it. Not only does this ensure that the buyer is protected if something happens to the item during shipping, it also protects you as the seller. The flat rate boxes and envelopes come with insurance up to a certain dollar amount. If the item sells for above that amount, I will personally pay the few extra dollars on the insurance to make sure my buyer and myself are protected from mail tragedies.

Take it back if it's not up to standards

Stand behind your item. If you didn't mention something that could affect a buyer's decision in your listing, don't be afraid to refund your buyer after you receive you item back. Pay for the return shipping as well. The buyer will see that you're a seller with integrity and that will help you gain rapport on eBay.

In the end, you want to make your buyer happy. If they're happy, they will positive feedback for you on eBay. The more positive feedback you receive, the better listing offers you will get from the website and the more buyers will be drawn to your items. Have integrity and make sure that you're taking care of your customer. Sometimes the demands might seem unfair, so knowing where to draw the line is important. Do whatever you can to make your buyer happy!

Chapter 7- Helpful Tips for Continued Selling Success

Congratulations! You have just sold your first item of clothing using eBay. While the feeling might be exhilarating at the moment, the success lasts for a short time if you don't keep up on your business. Knowing how to sell your items and making money is great, but what happens once you finish the transaction? In this chapter, I'm going to give you some tips and ideas on how to continue to make money selling garage sale and thrift store clothing on eBay. Once you get a feel for the business, it will become natural and you will become a power seller!

Continue to shop

Just because you found some great items during your first thrift store or garage sale run doesn't mean that these items are going to sell the way you hoped. They might not even sell at all. The point is, businesses are constantly getting new inventory that they can sell. You, too, need to make sure that you keep stocking up your personal inventory. Inventories and thrift stores are constantly changing, so you may not see the same item twice. Garage sales last a few days. Make time on a weekly basis to go around to your favorite thrift stores and look through the clothing. It might be a tedious task, but if it's a part of your routine, it will get easier and you will begin to find it becomes a habit.

Leave feedback for your buyer

Once the sale is complete on eBay, make sure that you're returning feedback to the buyer. Buyers like to receive positive feedback just as much as the seller does. Be honest when leaving your feedback. If they were difficult to work with, let other sellers know that. You want to make the buyer know how you felt about the experience as well. Maybe they did not realize that they were being difficult. However, before you post this for the public to see, let the buyer know in private.

Try new things

If you find that you're methods didn't get you as much money as you hoped to receive, try new things. Once you find your niche, you will be able to sell your items like a pro without much effort. Try taking your pictures in different ways, using different and unique ways to describe your items, and different ways to list the items. By gaining ideas from other sellers, you can make your own successful methods for selling your clothing. Another good thing to try is visiting thrift stores and garage sales in different parts of the city. Each demographic area will have different offerings and they might surprise you.

Ask your former buyers for advice

More than likely, your eBay buyers have purchased clothing from the website in the past. They know what to look for, what to buy, and what they want to see in a seller. Don't be afraid to ask them for advice on your listings or recommend items to them that you think they might like. The buyers will be flattered that you're taking the time to gain their insights on your business.

These are just a few tips that might help you in setting up a successful eBay selling business. Just because you find initial success doesn't mean that there isn't room for improvement. Take time to think of ways to make your items stand out and sell more frequently. Things change, so you need to move with the flow. Change can be good, and knowing what people like to buy is a huge plus to making sure you're making the big bucks by using eBay to sell the clothing you bought at a deep discount yourself!

Conclusion

I hope this book was able to help you to learn how to shop and resell thrift store and garage sale clothing items for a profit on eBay. While there's a common misconception that clothing sold on garage sales or in thrift stores are low quality and cheap, you might just find that there is an opportunity knocking at your door. People often donate used clothing without the thought that they might be worth more than they're asking. By taking the time to go through the massive amounts of clothing on the racks, you are potentially capitalizing on an underappreciated resource!

The next step is to try your hand and finding quality clothing that you think you can resell on eBay. Take some time and go around to the thrift stores and stop at garage sales to see if you can find something you'll be able to make extra money off of. You never know, you might be holding a treasure in your hand that everyone else has overlooked. After finding items you can potentially sell, take some time and get to know eBay and the ins and outs of selling there. I want to wish you luck on your venture to turn thrift store and garage sale clothing into huge profits!

Finally, if you enjoyed this book, then I'd like to ask you for a favor, would you be kind enough to leave a review for this book on Amazon? It'd be greatly appreciated!

THRIFT STORE RESELLING SECRETS YOU WISH YOU KNEW

50 Different Items You Can Buy At Thrift Stores And Sell On  And Amazon For Huge Profit

RICK RILEY

Introduction

This book contains proven steps and strategies on how to know what you should look for in the thrift stores and flip for big money on eBay and Amazon.

If you are looking into purchasing items from thrift stores and reselling them on Amazon or eBay, you need all of the information in this book. In this book you are going to find all of the top items that you need to keep your eye out for when you are thrift shopping. These items are going to bring in a large profit for you and most of them are not difficult to find.

You are also going to be given tips about how to make your listings work for you and how you can make sure you earn a profit from all of the items you are listing. Finally, you are going to learn what mistakes you don't want to do while you are learning to flip thrift store items.

Chapter 1
The Right Strategy to Get Started
Reselling

Before I start teaching you about all of the things you can purchase at a thrift store and sell on Amazon or eBay for a profit, I want share with you some important information. You shouldn't plan on just going to the thrift shop, grabbing a few items, listing them and making a profit. If you are going to make money selling the items you find at a thrift store on Amazon or Ebay, you need to first know what you are looking for! I am going to help you with that. Second, you need to understand that most people who do this work at it full time, often spending more than 40 hours a week on it.

The next thing that you need to know is that often times you can go digging through all of the stuff at thrift stores, spending your entire day searching and come home with nothing. So it can be difficult at times. It all depends on being at the right place at the right time.

You also need to weed out the pointless thrift shops, the ones that price things so high you will not be able to make a profit. For example, I found a leather jacket in good condition last week. The store wanted $50 for it but the most I could sell this for would be $60 and chances are I wouldn't even make that much. Small profits are not going to keep you going if you really want to get into this business. On the other hand, if you watch for sales at these stores you will be able to get much bigger profits. You see, the next day that same leather jacket was on sale for $25. This gave me a much better chance at making a profit. It was sold on eBay for $58.43.

So don't go into a thrift shop determined to find something. You have to be patient and if someone purchases your items before they go on sale, don't sweat it.

For the first item, I want to talk about brand names. You would expect that all known name brands would sell great, but that is not the case.

1. Item number one is Diesel Viker Mens jeans. You can sell these for a fairly good profit on eBay as well as Amazon if you can find them. One such sale was finding them for $6 at the thrift store and selling them for a little over $60. You do need to make sure they are in good condition and have all of the buttons and zippers. Always remember when inspecting clothing in the thrift store, try and find an area with good lighting so you can clearly inspect the piece of clothing you are thinking about buying.

2. Video games. There are tons of gaming systems, but what you want to look for is the older video games. Stuff like Super Mario Bros for Nintendo or Waterworld for Atari 2600. Game boy games sell great too. Rare games can often sell for $150 and can be purchased for about a buck at thrift stores. It is important that you look at the packaging because a game that would sell for $200 in good packaging will only sell for about $50 in torn packaging. Of course if it has never been opened it is worth more! In addition, always be on the lookout for prototype games for any system. These are games that are often extremely rare as they are in an unfinished state yet sometimes they slip through the cracks and end up in the thrift stores. These types of games can bring in huge amounts of profit!

3. As far as shirts go you want to focus on Polo shirts in the big and tall sizes. Remember that in general, the crazier and louder the design, the higher dollar amount it will usually sell for. These will sell quickly and you will be able to make a good profit on them. Most thrift stores will sell them for around $2 each and you can easily sell them for $20. In addition, always be on the lookout for vintage mens hawaiian shirts. If you see a vintage hawaiian shirt from the late 50's through early 70's, be sure to do some research on it by looking at the completed listings on eBay. Some of these early hawaiian shirts can bring in massive money. In general, the more vibrant the design, the more money you can count on coming your way in profits!

4. Shoes are an item that many people overlook, but it is something you really need to consider looking at to resell. If you can find Adidas, Nike or Trek shoes, you can usually purchase them for a couple of bucks and make about $50 - $75 per pair. You need to make sure they are in good condition, check the tread and the inside of the shoe. The older the shoe is, the more you can make off of it. Watch for shoes from the 70's and 80's. Keep an eye out for vintage Vans and Converse shoes.

5. Cassette tapes, VHS tapes, Disney movies still in the original packaging. Let's start with the cassette tapes and VHS tapes. These can be any brand and need to be blank and in the original packaging. In fact, any obsolete media can be sold on eBay and Amazon for a profit as long as they have not been used and are in the original packaging! These are very easy to find and you can purchase them fairly cheap usually a few bucks for a set. Disney movies on VHS tape are also a great way to make money. Anything that was made in the 90's or

earlier will sell usually sell quickly. If you find a thrift shop that has VHS tapes in their original box, you have found a gold mine. The great thing about these tapes is that they are easy to ship and don't take up a lot of space. You can also purchase them for about a 50 cents. Peter Pan is selling for about $3 while Davy Crockett is selling for about $15. This is a great return on your investment and can be a quick flip.

Chapter 2
Get a Smart Phone and Start Making Money

No matter how many items I list in this book, there are always going to be items in the thrift shops that you will come across and not know if they have any value. Even if you don't think the item has value, you still need to go ahead and use your cell phone to look it up on either eBay or Amazon. If you find that you can make at least 3x the investment price on either site you need to pick it up.

For example there was a flour mill at one of the thrift shops I frequently go to, it was priced at $20. To me that is a little high for a thrift shop, but I decided to look it up and found I could list it for $250 and turn it into a profit quickly. Of course I bought it but had I not had my smart phone I would have passed it by.

6. Toys!!! There are so many different toys that you can find that can earn you a ton of money. To start off we are going to talk about toy guns. This is a place where you can earn a great return, but you need to understand some thrift stores know what they have and won't sell them cheaply. One of the toy guns that is going for about $100 right now is a 1960's Lone Ranger Winchester rifle cap gun. If you find any toy guns from the 60's you are going to be able to make this kind of money, but watch for Winchester replicas. The price of this gun at a thrift shop is about $10 giving you a $90 profit.

7. Marx figurines are also something you need to keep your eye out for. It does not matter if they are plastic or metal. These sell quickly and you can make a great profit on them. One plastic figurine can be purchased for less than a $1 and easily sold for $10. A Popeye figurine is worth over a thousand dollars!

8. Vintage bobble head dolls are another thing you need to be on the lookout for. A set of Beetles bobble head dolls can go for as much as $5,000 and only cost about $100 at a thrift store. Any bobble head from the 60's that is in good condition can bring you a ton of money.

9. Vintage Lincoln Logs turn up in thrift stores all the time. The great thing about these is that you don't have to have a set or a box even, a simple mixed lot of Lincoln Logs can bring in $150 easily.

10. Books are not going to get you a ton of money unless you can find vintage Betty Crocker cookbooks. The older the better and they need to be in good to mint condition. Make sure all of the pages are there and they are not written on or stained.

11. Another book you need to watch out for is old Disney coloring books. They usually sell for about a quarter and you can sell them for up to $10. You need to make sure that again, all of the pages are there and they have not been scribbled on. Some will still sell if they have a few pages colored but I try to avoid these all together.

12. College books are another great item to keep an eye out for. If you live near a college town make sure to check out the thrift stores there. When purchasing college books, don't pay more than a few dollars and make sure they have any computer disks needed with them. You can easily get $20 -$30 for these books on Amazon or Ebay.

13. Tupperware is the next item I want to discuss. You need to make sure that it is real Tupperware and is in good condition. Wash it well before you take a photo of it to post and list any stains or issues with the Tupperware.

14. Anything Peanuts. All things Charlie Brown sell quickly and for a good price. Recently I saw a Peanuts doll sell for over a grand on eBay. Even the Peanuts sheet sets sell quickly.

15. Another toy to watch out for is Hulk Smash Hands. I consistently see these at thrift stores for $1 per set and they are selling for between $15 and $25 per set on eBay.

Chapter 3
Always Have a Plan B

If you purchase an item and it doesn't sell, what are you going to do with it? Do you have an area to store items while they sit on your store shelf or do you want to hold a garage sale and try to get rid of them that way? One thing that you don't want to do is donate them back to the store you bought them from. Even if you paid a quarter for it, do whatever you can to at least earn that quarter back. Allowing yourself to lose money no matter how small is not a habit you want to get into.

16. Hand held games are the next item. There are games like Yahtzee, Bridge and Nintendo Crystal Balloon Fight that sell anywhere between $40 and $300 depending on the rarity of the game. These were very popular in the 90's and even though they can be hard to find, they are worth the few bucks you will pay for them. Always be on the lookout for vintage Nintendo game and watch handheld systems. These were popular in the early 80's and always fetch a pretty penny on eBay.

17. Old electronics sell for just a few dollars at thrift stores and if you find brands like Sony or Panasonic, you can make quite a bit of money off of them. You need to make sure they are in fairly good condition and ensure they have all of the cords with them. If they do not have the cords find out how much it is going to cost to get replacement cords before purchasing the item.

18. Children's clothes sell great as well but you need to watch for brand names. Gymboree and Hanna

Anderson are some of the best selling brands of children's clothing and of course you need to make sure it is not stained or snagged. You also shouldn't pay more than $3 for these items if you want to make any type of profit.

19. Raggedy Ann and Andy dolls are an item I see a lot of at thrift stores but even though you can sell these for up to $100, you need to be very careful and only purchase the originals. Spending $30 on a set of 1990 Raggedy Anne and Andy dolls is not going to get you any money, as a matter of fact that is about all they are worth.

20. Large plush toys sell for upwards of $100 as well. You want to watch for plush toys such as Wily Coyote or Scooby Doo. The bigger they are, the more money they will go for. This is one item many people overlook.

21. Any World War 2 toys will pull in a huge profit as well. Always make sure they are authentic and in good condition before purchasing.

22. Pokémon! Anything Pokémon will sell. There are Pikachu plush toys, key chains and even Nintendo games. If you can find Pokémon items still in their package, you are going to be able to make a lot of money. Many of the Nintendo DS Pokémon games still have a high resale value.

23. I want to end this chapter by talking about Star Wars items and Barbie Dolls. If the Star Wars items are still in their original package you should invest in them. If they are not, go ahead and pass them up because you will not see much profit, unless the Stars Wars toys are early 80's and authentic. Barbie is something that so many people think is going to make them a lot of money, but unless you find the original Barbie in her

box, you are not going to make much of a profit. eBay and Amazon are saturated with Barbie sellers, so right now it is best to avoid them.

Chapter 4
Look For the Odd and Unusual

You need to watch for things that are not often found when it comes to thrift shopping. You need to look for anything that is odd or rare. When I saw a 1911 cathedral radio at a thrift store, it did not catch my eye because I knew what I was looking at. Instead it caught my eye because it was odd and I had never seen it before. You can purchase items like a bread maker at thrift stores all day long. This means they have very little resale value. However, finding something that you don't normally see like a 1911 radio is where you will make the most money.

24. That brings us to radios. You don't want to purchase just any radio when you are shopping. Keep your eye out for Philco radios. These are old antique radios that contain tubes. I purchased one for $25 because I liked the way it looked. I was going to keep it for myself until I found out I could sell it for $450.

25. Original Nintendo Systems will sell for a ton of money as well. The more games you can sell with the system the more money you will get. You also want to watch for extra remote controllers as well as the gun for Duck Hunt. If you ever see original NES Nintendo games sealed, always pick them up. You can make a ton of money selling sealed vintage games. When researching NES Nintendo games, always check the completed listings on eBay. If you find a game in the thrift shop and you are unsure of its resale value, take a quick look at the completed listings on eBay. This will give you all the information you need to decide whether or not it will be a profitable item for you. Remember, if the game

comes with the original box and instructions, that is a sure sign that you have struck gold. Any NES Nintendo game that you can find complete, should bring in a very nice profit. Especially if you can get these games under $5.

26. Vintage posters also sell very well. If you can find Sonic the Hedgehog posters or a New Kids on the Block poster from the eighties you can sell them pretty quickly for about $10. I have regularly found music posters from 1980's new wave bands that have sold upwards of $50. Keep your eye out music posters from obscure bands from the 1980's.

27. Sony handheld camcorders are a great find. I have found several of these at thrift stores for $5 and they go from $50-$75 dollars each. They sell for more if they come with the original case. Check to make sure all of the components are there and that it works. You should also check for an instruction manual which will bring in even more money.

28. Keep an eye out for old sports Jerseys. You can easily find a Michael Jordan Chicago Bulls basketball jersey and purchase it for $7 then list it for $60 and sell it quickly. Make sure it is in good condition and doesn't smell musty. If the clothes you are selling smell musty and moldy, people will expect a refund. If you do find a great item that smells bad, simply washing it and using vinegar in the washing machine can work wonders. Always pay attention to the washing instructions on the care tag before washing.

29. Art is great to buy at thrift stores as well, if they get a lot of estate donations. If you are going to purchase art you need to know what you are looking for. For example you can find a Picasso print for $30 at a resale shop and

list it for a good profit, but if you don't know it is a Picasso print you could just pass it up.

30. To finish up this chapter I want to talk about one more item that many people overlook, coffee mugs. Certain coffee mugs are very collectable and you can sell them for $5-$25 dollars each depending on the brand. What you want to watch for is anything Disney and Starbucks. Also, coffee mugs with a very unique theme also do quite well and can net a nice profit.

Chapter 5
Expand Your Horizons

Don't just limit yourself to purchasing items at thrift stores. Try going to some estate sales and even flea markets. Another great way to make money is watch for clearance items at your local stores. End of season sales and after holiday sales will give you great deals if you don't mind holding on to items until next year. This is one reason why storage is so important when it comes to selling on eBay and Amazon.

31. Silver. I don't have a specific name brand for you here but trust me, you can find silver at thrift stores. It is often put on the shelf by mistake with the rest of the utensils so you need to know how to spot it! Now you may be thinking that no one is going to buy a spoon here or a fork here, but this is what they know that you need to know. Silver no matter what form it takes is still silver and people will buy this stuff!

32. Comic books can have great resale value. Especially old Marvel comic books that are in good condition. You need to make sure they are not damaged, that the pages are all there and if you can find them in mint condition you are going to make even more. You can sell comic books all day long online, so anytime you have the chance to pick them up do it.

33. Watch out for 80's GI Joes. Many of these can go for a couple hundred dollars. Even GI Joe parts sell for a lot more than you would expect, so keep your eyes out for them. Make sure they are real GI Joes and not something you would purchase from a dollar store.

34. Winter coats can also bring in some good money if you are willing to hold on to them if they do not sell immediately. You can easily find vintage Pendleton coats for $2 or $3 each and sell them for close to $100 during the winter time. If you find them at the end of the season you can get them and hold on to them until the next season. Always be on the lookout for Patagonia, North Face and Spyder jackets.

35. Remington adding machines. Up until this point we have talked mostly about items that are fairly light and not too difficult to ship, but an adding machine is much heavier. This weight and extra shipping costs do not seem to bother the buyers, in fact you can purchase one of these for $3-$5 at a thrift store and list it for $30 without a problem.

36. This one does not have a brand name but you should really keep an eye out for beads and jewelry making supplies. Many people are taking up jewelry making and beads are expensive! I found several strings of beads for a quarter a piece, took them off the string bagged them up and sold them for $5 each. Easy money and easy to ship.

37. Blood pressure machines sell regularly for $35 to $40 so if you can purchase one for $4 or $5 you can easily sell it for $20 on eBay or Amazon. One thing I like to do is carry a few AA batteries with me so that when I find these items, I can make sure they work before I spend my money on them.

38. Care Bears are an item that I love picking up. They have to be the original Care Bears from the 80's and you can usually get them for $1 each. They easily go for $20 to avid collectors.

39. Previously I said you should avoid most clothes, but if you can find concert T-shirts pick them up. These again

need to be from the 80's or earlier and you need to make sure it is not a replica, but once you do this you can earn some quick cash. You can usually pick up a T-shirt for $2 and sell them for as high as $75 depending on what concert tour it was from. An Aerosmith T-shirt can get you $50 while a Led Zeppelin can go for $125. There is huge money to be made selling vintage concert shirts. It is more difficult to find these shirts in the thrift shops these days. However, you can still find these treasures on the racks!

40. The last thing I want to talk to you about in this chapter is fur. There is no brand name for this one, as long as it is real fur and it is cheap buy it. I want to make it clear that if the store knows what they have, they will mark the price up. I went to a resale shop that advertised they had received a lot of new fur coats in, they priced them at over $500 each. On the other hand if you are just going through a store and find a fur coat for a few dollars, do not pass it up. Check to make sure it is real fur. This will be marked on the tag and you can often smell them to make sure it is real. This next tip is very important. Check the lining and make sure that if it is loose, you can have it fixed fairly cheap. Be ready for it to sell fast! Even though many people are protesting 'new' fur, they have no problem buying old fur and actually prefer it.

Chapter 6
Be Consistent and Stay Focused

Hopefully the advice that I have given you at the beginning of each of these chapters has helped you, but what I am going to tell you now could be the most important advice I could ever give you. List regularly and list often! If you do not list often you are going to see your listings dropping down and not getting seen by most people. The same thing is going to happen if you do not list regularly. This will cause you to see a drop in sales.

I am not saying you have to list 30 items a day, but if you go out and purchase 10 items don't list them all at once. List one each day and then plan a new trip to get more items. You will see your sales grow if you list regularly and often.

41. Harry Potter books. I did mention earlier that most books won't sell, but if you do see Harry Potter books you need to pick them up. Set them to the side and hold onto them watching out for more each time you shop. Once you have a complete set, list it and watch how much you can sell it for. If you want to get the most profit possible, I suggest not paying more than a couple of bucks per book, even better purchase on days when books are marked down to a quarter!

42. Figurines are always for sale at thrift shops, but you need to keep an eye out for Holly Hobby. Most of the figurines you will find are going to be worthless but Holly Hobby sells very well. Flip the figurine over and look for the Holly Hobby label on the bottom. Of course, just like with almost everything, you are going

to be purchasing at thrift stores, you don't want to pay more than a few bucks for each one and you want to make sure there are no cracks or chips in the figurines.

43. Another strange item you can make money with is JC Pennies and Sears catalogs. Many people will remember getting these each year at about Christmas time, and for some reason they want to purchase them today. Call it remembering their childhood if you must, but for whatever reason they are willing to pay up to $25 for a catalog you can find at a thrift store for about $2.

44. As you can see, there are many great items that sell and many odd items. I don't know whether to say this item is odd or cute, or really what to call it, but novelty ties are a huge seller. You can purchase these for about 50 cents each and sell them for up to $15. You should watch for ties with themes such as The Simpsons, McDonalds, Disney, and Garfield. Of course there are tons and tons more ties that will sell, remember look for the rare items.

45. Costumes for your pets is another item you should keep your eyes out for. You can get these very cheap during the Halloween season and sell them all year long. People love to dress up their pets and for some reason dog bridal gowns sell really well. These do not have to be any specific brand but you need to make sure they are in good condition and clean.

What is going to make you successful when it comes to buying from thrift shops and selling on eBay and Amazon? Timing. We have all heard it but timing really is everything. If you find an item that is selling quickly that you can make a good profit on, sell it now. Don't slack off and not list the item.

One story was of a seller who listed an RC airplane that he purchased for $25 at a thrift store. He sold it for over $300 and just six months later another seller couldn't get more than $50 for the one he had listed.

This happens all the time. What is hot today may not be hot tomorrow and you need to stay on top of your game! List your items and if the prices drop, don't get rid of your items. Remove the listing and simply hold on to the item until the prices go up again.

Patience is key when it comes to selling on eBay and Amazon. Your first listing is going to seem like it is taking forever if you just sit there and watch it. I know a lady who posted her first listing and literally sat there watching each bid be put in. She was miserable. Then I also know of a guy who posted his listing, left it alone for two days and was amazed to see that he earned $150 dollars from it.

List the items and leave it alone. Don't sit there and torture yourself for hours at a time watching the bids come in.

You also need to consider the amount of money that eBay, Amazon and PayPal are going to charge you. Carefully examine all of the listing and closing fees for the eBay item category you are listing in. Also, make sure you are aware of the PayPal fees as well. This is why I told you that you should not mess with an item unless you are sure you are going to make at least 3-5 times the amount of money you have in it.

Chapter 7

Set Your Goals and Make a Plan

Too often I have seen people jump into thrift shop flipping and not have a plan or any goals which of course leads to failure. So set up your goals, but don't get all crazy about the amount of money you want to make. It is very possible to make $1,000 dollars a month flipping part time but you are not going to make this starting out.

I was talking to a friend who was very interested in getting into flipping, but when they tried they wanted to make $1,000 a month. The first month they listed their items and made over $400 but became disappointed because they did not reach their goals.

I was so amazed that they were disappointed because I saw it as a win, they on the other hand did not. I had to explain to them that they needed to allow themselves time to work up to the goal of $1,000 dollars per month. So make sure you start with an obtainable goal that will pay for the time you spend flipping.

Now to finish up with the final five items you need to watch for when thrift shopping.

46. Puff the Magic Dragon is such a favorite for so many people. I remember when I got mine when I was a kid and how much I loved him. Once I grew up and learned about Puff, I wished I had not lost him all of those years ago. Now think about how many other people are out there wishing they still had their Puff and looking for a new one. As a matter of fact you can find one of these for just a couple of bucks and sell them for $30 each.

47. Scrabble tiles are once again of the odd things that sell online and that you can get for next to nothing. I actually have a deal with several thrift stores, they save all of the loose Scrabble tiles they find for me and I keep them from going in the garbage. Once a month I make my rounds and pick up tiles. Depending on how any you can collect, you can sell them for between $10 and $100 so it is important to get as many as you can.

48. Disney characters. We all know you can get money for selling Mickey and Minnie mouse items. However, you can also turn a good profit with Pluto, Donald Duck, even fining a Flounder toy from the movie The Little Mermaid can make you $15. You should watch for plush toys, posters, small plastic toys, anything that is Disney.

49. Remember the Walk Man CD players from the 90's? These are a great seller. I find these all the time at thrift stores for $4 or $5 each and they sell for between $25 and $50 each. You want to try and get the ones that are still in the packaging if you want to make the most money, but don't pass up the ones that are not still in the original packaging because you can still make money on them with no problems. Use those batteries I told you to carry around with you and test the Walk Man to make sure it works. It is also good to have a CD available to test out if possible, as well as a set of ear buds because not all Walk Men are going to come with these items. You want to make sure you are not wasting your money on broken items.

50. Portable typewriters, the typewriters that you don't have to plug in. These are one of my favorite items to purchase and resell. They can be purchased for about $5 each and sell at about $60 or more. I find these all of the time. I actually found 7 in one day!

There are so many items that you can purchase at a thrift store and resale for a profit on eBay and Amazon. There is no way I can go over every item in this book, but when you are out and you are shopping at thrift stores you need to remember what I have mentioned several times in this book. Look for the odd, the obscure and the rare. If you see something you have never seen before look it up on your smart phone! You can easily use eBay to judge what the value of the item you are looking at is.

There you have it 50 items that you can go out and look for in your local thrift stores right now, but don't limit yourself to just the local thrift stores. Make sure you look for a few in some upscale neighborhoods, this is where you are going to find the best items. Don't forget to look at estate sales, yard sales and even storage unit auctions. Look everywhere you can to find great used items for your listings.

But remember to take it slow. Don't start out spending 40 hours a week doing this and investing $500 a week. Start with about $30-$40 to invest, turn a profit and get your money out of it. After that you can work with the profit to earn more and more!

Conclusion

I hope this book was able to help you to understand that there are tons of items you can purchase at thrift stores and flip on eBay and Amazon.

The next step is to decide how much you want to invest, set your goals and get to the nearest thrift store!

Thrifting and Winning

and

Winning

50 WAYS TO MAKE MONEY BUYING ITEMS AT THRIFT STORES AND SELLING THEM FOR HUGE PROFITS

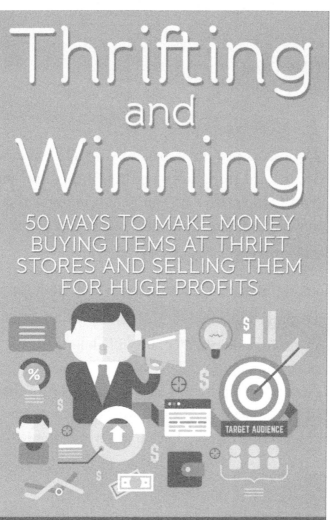

RICK RILEY

Introduction

This book contains proven steps and strategies on how to find items in your local thrift store and resell them for maximum profits. Thrift stores are a treasure chest of items that are just waiting to be found. For some, it's only junk, but for others, it can be a gold mine.

When looking at a thrift store, don't look at it as someone else's used junk, but look at it as a way to find treasures to make you extra money. People will donate items that are worth tons of money on a daily basis. Why not capitalize on these treasures? This book will help you to find these items and sell them in such a way that you can make tons of cash from your local thrift store. Let's make some money!

Chapter 1- Thrift Stores: A World of Possibility

If you're like a lot of people, you might view thrift stores as a place where people recycle their used junk. Much of these items are old and damaged, but someone will be able to use them, right? You may not realize that you can actually find some wonderful treasures in the aisles of these stores. People give away items that they may not know are valuable on a daily basis. If they are uninformed about what they hold in their hands, it's their loss and your gain.

Being able to find items in the thrift store that are worth money will take some time and research. Since not many people take the time to know what they have within their possession you can definitely use your knowledge to benefit you financially. Just think of what you can find within the walls of your local thrift store if you would have the time and the knowledge to find out!

Now that you know that your local thrift store is a great place to make some money, it's time to figure out what you can find there that will earn you that extra cash. Learning what people are looking for and would spend money on will help you get the edge on finding the items and making top dollar on them.

If you're still uncertain as to what this would look like, don't worry. We will take a look at the top items for you to look for as well as methods to ensure that you are getting the most money from them.

Millions of items go through thrift stores on a daily basis that the people buying and donating them don't have any clue as to what their true worth is. With an opportunity like this, why not take advantage of the lack of knowledge in this area? By educating yourself and knowing what you as an individual can look for when thrift store shopping, you can potentially earn major cash by finding the right items in your local thrift store!

Looking at your thrift store in a different light will give you some inspiration and excitement to get started on this venture. You may have some difficulties to begin with, but once you get started, you will find that you will develop a method for finding what you can make the most money on and finding the best way to earn this money.

Let's get started on tips for finding thrift store items to resell for big money! This might be the way you can make extra income that you have been searching for!

Chapter 2- What to Look for in Thrift Stores that is Worth Money

If you have not had many experiences with thrift stores, the thought of suddenly going into them and trying to find something of worth can be like trying to search for a needle in a haystack. The size of most thrift stores can make it an all-day venture if you don't know what you're looking for and how you can cut corners to find it. Taking the time to know what you can find in your thrift store will ultimately save you time when you walk through the doors and see just how much stuff is on the shelves.

What can you find in a thrift store to make you some extra money? That is probably the burning question in your mind right now. Getting started might take a little time, but once you have learned the methods for finding what you can use, you will begin to find a system that will work well for you.

Look for Top Brands

Every genre of items has a popular brand name label. From clothing to electronics, there will be brands that will stand out from the rest of the pack. Knowing which brands are the top brands and how much they are really worth can help you to search through the shelves and racks with a more scrutinizing eye. You are not looking for aesthetically pleasing items as much as you are looking for who made them. Top brands will often sell for more money than their less popular counterparts, so keep that in mind as you do your searching and research.

Look at the Age of the Item

Older looking items can be either well used or antiques. Knowing when you find an antique can help you to find items that will be collectable amongst a certain crowd. Since many older items are no longer made, when people come across them, they will want to purchase them for their collections. If you are going in search of antique or collectable items, know what you're looking for and know that antiques can look older in respect to other items that you might encounter.

Look at the Material the Item is Made From

The materials that items are made of can help to determine their value. Higher quality and rarer materials are worth more than cheaper made materials. For example, if you're looking at figurines, the ones that are made with porcelain will be worth more than the ones that are made of simple clay. By knowing the difference in these materials, you can pick out what you would believe to be higher valued items from those that are not worth much at all.

Know What is Popular

Even if the item may seem silly and not worth the time to look at, it may be incredibly popular amongst a group of collectors. Kids will have fads that you think are ridiculous, but those who are a part of the fad will pay top dollar to get whatever the fad requires. Take a look at current trends and try to find items that will fit into the popular trends. They can make you much more money than not knowing what people out there are looking for.

Search Online Websites to See What is in Demand

Along with knowing what is popular, you can use your resources to find what people are looking for. The internet is a wonderful resource. You can look on the popular auction and sales websites to see what people are actually buying. This can help guide you when you go into a thrift store and have no idea where you would like to begin.

Learn to Look After the New Merchandise is Put Out

Thrift stores will have certain times when they will move their new inventory out to the sales floor. This is a prime time to look at what they have to offer because not too many people have had the chance to look through it before you get there. This will help you to have a better chance at finding the best items you can sell without having to do a lot of digging.

Visit Multiple Stores

Different areas and neighborhoods will have different types of items donated to their thrift stores. By looking in multiple thrift stores in different areas, you will get to see a better array of what the thrift store world can offer you. If you have extra time, try going to the different areas within your city or another nearby city and see what you can find!

Look Behind the Items in Front

With so many donations being dropped off, some of the items will get pushed back on the shelves to make room for the new items. By taking the time to look at the items that have been pushed to the back, you can find some treasures that people will pass by because they will just look at the items in front.

Scrutinize Grab Bags Carefully

When there are a lot of items that serve a similar purpose, such as office supplies, thrift stores will often combine these into bags and sell the entire bag at a certain price. Valuable items can be tucked in these grab bags because the employees who put them together may not know what they have in their hands is really valuable. It might take a little extra time, but finding the treasure in a grab bag can be totally worth it.

By knowing where to get started and what to look for in a thrift store, you will be better prepared to go in and find the items that can be useful to you. Before going into the store, try looking around and finding out what items are valuable and what brands are in demand. You can save yourself a lot of time and frustration by doing just a little research before going in!

Chapter 3- Finding Websites and Other Venues to Sell Your Goods on

Once you have found the items in the thrift stores, it's time to make the next move and sell your finds to the people who will want them. However, there are different ways in which you can sell these items. Some ways will earn you more money than others, so knowing which ways to sell certain items will help you to get the most out of the items that you have found.

Where can you sell used items? How can you find the customers who will pay top dollar for what you have? These are the questions that you might be asking yourself at this very moment. Don't worry, you're not the only one! Let's take a look at the different ways you can sell your thrift store finds for the most money.

eBay

eBay is the top auction website on the internet. Anyone can buy or sell on this site, and many people will turn to this site first when looking for items that they are seeking. However, some items will sell better in this setting than others. Collectibles and popular items are huge sellers on this website. Think about selling items such as toys, trading cards, and unique figurines when selling on eBay. The bidding will work the price up and you may be surprised with how much your item will sell for in the end.

Amazon

Amazon is another popular site where sellers can offer their wares. This site is set up with you choosing how much you would like the buyer to purchase your item for. In order to do that, you will need to know what your item is worth and not overpricing it. Also, you will want to ensure that you are pricing it with its condition in mind. Many people will turn to Amazon to look for used books and music. You may find that other items that you have found will sell well in this setting too.

Antique Stores

If you're dealing with items that are older and may be out of production, an antique store may be the place to sell your finds in. Large antique shops operate by renting out areas where people can set up their own shops. In order for this to be a possibility, you will want to have a wide array of items that would be considered antique. If you don't then you may want to consider partnering with another seller and renting a booth together.

Craft Fairs

If you are dealing with items that can be considered crafty, such as wall art or quilts, then a craft fair could be a great way to get top dollar for your items. Again, like an antique store, craft fairs are operated in booths, so you will want to make sure that you have more than a few items to sell in order to make this worth your while.

Craigslist

Even though many people are afraid of buying and selling on Craigslist, you can actually make a decent amount of money on this site if you're careful and know how to avoid fraud and dangerous situations. This is a good site to sell the larger items on, so think about using it if you find high quality furniture that you know that someone will be looking for.

Etsy

If you don't have enough merchandise to sell at a craft fair, Etsy is the craft fair's online counterpart. You can individually list your items on this website and sell as few or as many items as you wish. This site operates much like Amazon, except it deals with handmade goods. So, if you have a few crafty items you wish to sell and don't want to go through the hassle of a craft fair, consider opening an using an Etsy account to sell them!

Social Media

Many social media sites have groups that have come together to buy and sell in certain areas and certain types of items. You can easily search these groups and find one that your items would fit into and ask to join the group. After admitted, you can post your items and sell it to the people within the group.

Knowing where you can sell your items and which ways to sell your items will ensure that you get the best price for what you sell. Before posting or setting out your items, take a look at what the store or the site has to offer. If you see that similar items sell well in one area and not in another, go with the best way to sell what you have. You can also use several of the methods to sell different types of items. The more you understand about where to sell, the better chance you have of making a better profit.

Chapter 4- Learning to Ask the Appropriate Price

One of the biggest mistakes that new sellers make is not pricing their goods appropriately. Some will severely overprice their items and no one will purchase them, or the seller will underprice the item and take a small profit or a loss from what they sell. Knowing how to find the best price for your items will take some research, but knowing what you can get for what you have will benefit you in the long run.

How do you price used items? You might feel awkward pricing something that you just purchased used. Why would anyone buy something used from you? You would be surprised at how well used items really do sell. In this chapter, I'm going to give you some tips on how to price your items just right to make sure you get the best profits from your items.

Search the Web for Similar Items

Since the internet is a great way to find out information, use it to your benefit. When going onto the internet to research which method would be best for selling your item, look at the asking prices of other sellers. This can give you a general idea of how much the item can sell for. Also, you can look and see what similar items have already sold for on some of the sales websites. Gather this information and use it when pricing your own item. You want to ask a fair price without asking too much or too little.

Use Antique Pricing Catalogs

If you're dealing with antiques, pricing guides can be a wonderful resource for you when pricing what you wish to sell. These guides will tell you how much the item will sell for by year and condition. The prices given are the average price that you can buy them for, so if you price what you're selling within those limits, you should be able to get a good price for what you're selling.

Find a Good Pricing Guide

Pricing guides are out there for almost anything that you wish to buy or sell. Find the appropriate and most up to date guides and use them as a reference when selling your items. These guides are written by the experts, so you know that the advice is reliable and that you won't get taken advantage of.

Look for Trends in Pricing

As time goes on, some items will change in popularity and demand, therefore changing how much you can sell it for. If the price of what you're selling takes a dive, you don't want to keep asking that high of a price for it. Lower or raise your price according to what the current pricing trends are.

Note the Item's Condition When Pricing

When dealing with used merchandise, there is always the question of the item's physical condition. Your buyers will want to know what that condition is when you sell it. If it's not in factory packaging, you need to give as much detail about the item as you can, and you need to let the price that you're asking for the item reflect that item's condition.

Price Competitively

In order to actually sell your item, you don't want to ask top dollar for it. You want to entice the buyers to purchase what you're selling. So, price your item like the other ones of the same condition, but make buyers come to yours because you can give them the best price. This is a good idea, especially if you're dealing with an auction website or another website that expects you to sell your item in a certain time frame.

If Auctioning, Start Low

When using sites such as eBay, start your initial bid low and let the buyers work it up for you. If you start with a minimum bid that is too high, then people will find similar items to bid on instead. People will want to get the cheapest price for what you have to sell, and if they feel if they can get that elsewhere, your item may not sell at all.

Pricing your items is an incredibly important element of getting the most out of your thrift store finds. Finding a good price and having people think that it is reasonable are the best ways to ensure that you sell what you want for what it is really worth. Don't allow the buyers to dictate the price if you know that it is worth more than they are willing to pay. It might just mean that you have to find a different way to sell it.

Chapter 5- Know When You're Being Taken Advantage of

As I have mentioned before, you want to sell your item for top dollar, and your buyer wants to purchase it for as little as possible. When these factors come into play, you can easily fall into the buyer's hand. However, you can counteract the problem by knowing what the true value of your item is, and you can know what you can reasonably sell it for. There will be people out there who will try to get you to sell it to them for less. Some of them can be very convincing. You can combat these types of people by knowing how to stand up for yourself in the selling world.

How confident are you that you won't let people take advantage of you? If you feel like people do that in your life, it's time to look at ways that you can avoid being made a fool of and losing money instead of taking away a profit.

Know What Your Item is Truly Worth

By doing your research and knowing how to price your items fairly, you shouldn't have to haggle the price with a potential buyer. The price should sell it for what you want to sell it for. People will constantly try to get more for less, so stand up for yourself and don't let them get away with getting what you have to sell for less than you know you can sell it for.

Be Polite When Discussing Prices

You will get people who will want to discuss buying your item, but they will want to buy it for what they want to buy it for. If you know that what they are willing to give you is much less than what you know you can get for it, be polite and let them know that they can either purchase it for the asking price or not purchase it at all.

Be Aware of Private Messages on Sales Websites Concerning Pricing

If using an auction website, you might get private messages from bidders asking you to sell it to them for a certain price. While other bidders are honestly bidding on your item, someone is trying to get in and get it without having to deal with the competitive aspect of the site. More than likely, your auction price will get you more than this secret buyer is willing to pay. So, just be polite and let this buyer know that the item can be purchased by the highest bidder.

Stick to Your Price

If you know that the price that you have given your item is fair, then don't let anyone try to haggle it down. The item will sell for what you want it to if it is in demand and you have set a fair price on it. Remember, people are trying to get more for less, so don't fall victim to their whims. Stick to your price and don't let them tell you what you should sell it for. You have done your research and you're sticking to it!

Know When You Should Give in

Sometimes, no matter how well you price your item, it will not sell for what you wish it to sell for. This can be due to a number of reasons, but it is better to get something from your merchandise than not to be able to sell it at all. If you have a buyer who is interested and can give you what you at least paid for it, then give in and let that item go. It might just be that your item wasn't what you thought it was and you shouldn't waste any more time on it.

Don't Take Payments Outside of Cash or PayPal

There are a lot of scams out there. Sadly enough, people will use alternative methods of payment that are often fraudulent when purchasing items. Don't allow that to happen to you. When selling your items in person, accept only cash. You can verify if the cash is real by looking at its security features. If selling online, use a reliable third party, such as PayPal. They will protect you from cyber fraud.

Knowing a Scammer When You See One

Scammers can be smooth characters. They might seem like the nicest and most honest people, but that is a ploy to get what they want. Look for things that just don't fit when you're dealing with a potential buyer. Often times, your gut feeling can lead you to make the right decision regarding your sale.

Listen to your gut and don't sell it if the buyer seems off in any way. There will be other people out there who will buy what you have to sell.

Be Aware When Someone Offers You More Than You Know the Item is Worth

Sometimes, a scammer will try to give you more for what you're selling than what it is really worth. This is a way for them to get what you have to sell and also take advantage of you. When you try to tell them that they are offering too much, they will ask for you to send the extra money back. In reality, that money was bogus to start with.

Being taken advantage is not fun. When you're trying to be honest and make an honest income, getting scammed can really hurt. People will take advantage of you if given the chance. Even if you like to think the best of people, be careful. They might just be putting on an act to get what they want for what they want it for, and you will take the loss in the end.

Chapter 6- Learning to Find Opportunities in Your Community

Every community has different events and opportunities to buy and sell. While one community can be on the internet, another one can be your local church or charity group. Finding opportunities in your community to buy and sell will help you to make even more money. Even if you stick to thrift stores, you can find areas in your community that you can sell your finds in.

If you're looking for other opportunities to purchase items to sell for a profit, community events can also be a helpful place to start. Knowing your community and its offerings well can help you get an edge on making the most money from your finds! Don't limit yourself to just thrift stores. You can use other resources to find items that will earn you major cash right in your community. Your community can also help you with selling the items.

Church Garage Sales

Church garage sales are a prime place to find items of worth. You can navigate these much the same way as you would navigate a thrift store, and you can often get the price lower than what they want for it. Also, you are supporting the community by buying from an organization within the community. Garage sales also tend to ask lower prices of items than you would pay for them in a thrift store. If you can get it at a garage sale, you might get a better bargain and a better profit from your purchase in the end.

Community Garage Sales

A lot of housing developments and smaller towns often have one huge garage sale in which multiple people participate. This can give you the opportunity to walk around and find things that may not end up in the thrift stores. Just like a church garage sale, the owners might let you haggle them down on the price just to get rid of the items. Take advantage of this when going to the garage sales. You can use the same knowledge that you used for the thrift stores when wandering someone's garage sale.

Another great thing about garage sales is that people are bound and determined to get rid of their junk. They might take any price for it rather than having to load it and take it to the thrift store. Knowing the characteristics of garage sales can work to your advantage, especially if you know that the item that you are purchasing can earn you some major cash!

Local Antique Shops

Local antique shops could be a great way for you to sell your antiques that you purchased at the thrift store. They are looking for inventory too, and they wish to bring in customers. See if they are willing to give you a good price for the items that you are selling and allow them to deal with the retail end of the bargain.

Also, if you can build a relationship with a local antique shop owner, they might allow you to sell your items in their store for a small fee. When looking into this, you can make more money because you are not having to deal with people haggling you and you don't have to worry about paying shipping and handling fees for your items!

Message Boards

There might be areas in your downtown area where people can post their flyers and ads. Try using this method and post your item to sell it. This works out well in college areas because students like to look for unique and interesting items, so they will look at these message boards frequently.

Internal Message Boards

Some employers have a message board where their employees can post things that they wish to sell. If your employer has this type of deal, try using that and selling it through the message board. Odds are that you won't have to pay for shipping fees because that employee works in the same building as you do.

Finding community methods to buy and sell are becoming increasingly popular. From using social media to buy and sell to using the message board in the downtown area, you might be surprised at the money you can get for what you wish to sell.

Chapter 7- Keeping Up to Date on Items that Sell for Big Money

Times change. Along with time, prices of items and the ways in which they are sold will also change. It's important that you keep yourself educated and up to date on pricing trends and how they affect the items that you are trying to sell. It could be either good or bad when thrift store reselling is in the picture. However, you can keep yourself from taking some major losses if you know what to look for and how to work around it.

It is amazing how an item can change in popularity in a short amount of time. Once it becomes popular, everyone wants it, and once it loses its popularity, then no one wants it. However, there are items that will never lose their worth, and that is one area that you can focus on when buying and selling.

Don't be afraid to go research prices and selling prices often. Depending on what you're looking at, you may save yourself money by refraining from buying it in the first place. The great part about technology is that you can check the prices in real time while you're standing in front of the item in question. There are apps and websites that can be accessed through a mobile device that will tell you what the item is worth before you even take it to the cash register.

Going online before you go thrift store shopping is another way to find out what is selling at that moment in time. Knowing what you're looking for and what people are buying can be valuable when faced with a huge thrift store. Who knows, a certain type of item could be more popular today than it was just a week ago! Don't be left in the dust because you didn't take the time to do the research before you started shopping.

If you go thrift store shopping regularly, then you might want to keep up on the trends via your computer and online selling sites. They are the most reliable and up to date way to know what people are buying and how much they are paying for what they're buying.

Finally, don't be left behind because you're too busy to keep up on trends. You might just run into the right item at the right time. Knowing that this item can earn you big money will make your perseverance worth it!

Good luck on finding your items and selling them for the best price possible! You can do this!

Conclusion

I hope this book was able to help you to understand what an opportunity lies in the walls of your local thrift store. Earning money can be easy when you know what to look for and how to sell it to waiting buyers!

The next step is to do some research and find out what is popular today that you can make some big money on. Knowing that the thrift stores are a treasure chest, use them to help you gain that extra cash!

Finally, if you enjoyed this book, then I'd like to ask you for a favor, would you be kind enough to leave a review for this book on Amazon? It'd be greatly appreciated!

THRIFT STORE KNICK KNACKS INTO GIANT CASH STACKS

50 EVERYDAY ITEMS YOU CAN BUY CHEAP AT THRIFT STORES AND RESELL ON EBAY AND AMAZON FOR HUGE PROFIT

RICK RILEY

Introduction

This book contains proven steps and strategies on how to flip thrift store items and sell them for a profit on eBay.

This book is for anyone who wants to learn how they can purchase items from a thrift store and sell them for a profit on eBay and Amazon. All of the items listed in this book are guaranteed sellers. As you learn about the different items you should look for while you are shopping, you are also going to learn great tips and tricks that will help you be successful at flipping the items for huge profit!

You are going to learn about everyday items that are easy to find in any thrift store. You will also learn about generic categories as well as specific items that you should look for. In addition, you will learn how you can find items on your own that may not be listed in this book, but that you will still be able to sell for a profit.

Finally you will learn what you should do in order to make your business a success. By following the advice and tips in this book, you will be well on your way to making big time money reselling thrift store items on eBay and Amazon.

Chapter 1
Where to Begin and What to Buy

Deciding that you are going to start purchasing from thrift stores and reselling on eBay is a great business to get into, but it is just that, a business. Those who are successful at purchasing from thrift stores and reselling on eBay and Amazon can spend 40 to 60 hours a week shopping for and listing their items. They also have to spend time learning about each of their items and what the hottest selling items are.

You see, one day you may be able to get $30 for an item you purchased for $3 and the next day you may not be able to sell that same item at all. It all depends on how many people are selling that specific item on eBay. Throughout this book I am going to teach you which items you should look for while you are searching through thrift shops, as well as give you tips on how to ensure your success at selling on eBay and Amazon.

1. Clothing. Yes you can sell clothing on eBay, but you need to be very careful about the types of clothing you purchase from a thrift store. First you need to make sure there are no stains or snags, you need to check and make sure there are no buttons or zippers missing. The next thing you need to know is that not all clothes will sell on eBay. Watch for big and tall clothes for men, plus size clothing for women, name brand clothing and polo shirts. These are the types of adult clothes that sell the most. Always be on the lookout for vintage mens hawaiian shirts. You want to be looking for loud, vibrant hawaiian shirt designs.

Childrens clothing also sells very well but it needs to be a recognizable brand. You will not be able to sell childrens no name clothing no matter how great the condition is. Watch for brands like Old Navy or Gymboree when purchasing childrens clothing.

2. College books are also a great thing to keep an eye out for when you are shopping at a thrift store. If you live near a college town you can find tons of these super cheap, post them on eBay or Amazon and make a great profit! You do need to make sure the books are not written in and that they come with any computer software that is needed. Make sure they are in good condition and none of the pages are torn out. Students spend tons of money on these each year and many are turning to purchasing online, so if you can get some before the school year starts chances are you will make a great profit.

3. Keep your eye out for board games the next time you go to a thrift store. If you can find vintage board games that are still in good condition and contain all the pieces for the game you will make a profit off of it. One vintage game I always sell for huge profit is called Crossbows And Catapults.

4. Shoes are one item that many people overlook because they think there is no profit to be made, but if you can find name brand shoes from the 70's you will be able to purchase them for a few dollars and sell them for up to $50. Always buy vintage Converse and Nike shoes if they are in good condition and have a unique design.

5. Old telephones are a great item to keep your eye out for as well. Rotary telephones sell for $1-$2 at a thrift store

but you can make $30-$40 dollars on them when you list them on eBay. This is before shipping so you don't have to worry about shipping eating into your profits. All you need to do is make sure that the phones still work. Most thrift stores will have a sticker on items that say 'works'. If your store does not, then simply ask if it has been tested and if they will test it for you.

6. Toys are another item you should watch for. Now I am not saying you should go out and purchase a ton of junk toys from thrift stores, what I am saying is you should watch for specific toys. I regularly find vintage He-Man and Star Wars toys from the 1980's at garage sales.

   One warning I have for you though, you want to look for things that have slid by the workers at the thrift store. When the store knows what they have they will usually place it behind glass. For example, one store I went to had a Raggedy Ann and Andy dolls. They wanted $50 for them, knowing I could only sell them for about $30 a piece, it was not worth it for me to even consider purchasing them. The store knew they had an item that was worth something. If you find yourself in a thrift store wanting to buy something that is a bit out of your price range, but you know you can make a profit on, always ask to talk to the store manager. Many times they have worked the price down for me or I offer to make a package deal with other items. You never know until you ask!

7. Video games are something else you need to keep an out for. I was once wandering through a thrift store and saw a Zelda game for the Game Boy gaming system still in the box for $3. I got it, went home and sold it for $25

before shipping. It is items like this that you want to watch for, things that you will pay little for and that will sell quickly. Any Nintendo games, Game Boy games or even Atari games will sell quickly and for a great profit. The great thing about these is that they are easy to ship as well.

8. Black and white photographs. This is another item that many people over look but sells great on eBay! They are also super easy to ship. Don't ask me why black and white photographs sell so well, I would never be able to answer that. What I do know is that it does not matter who the photograph is of, all that matters is that it is in good condition and that it is an old photograph.

Those eight items are a great place to start when it comes to purchasing items from thrift stores and selling them on eBay and Amazon. My tip for you in this chapter is that you should always keep a smart phone with you so that if you do come across an item that you think may sell quickly on eBay, you will be able to check and see if you are going to be able to make a profit from it. Check to see what the item is currently selling for on eBay and how many people are actually selling the item. If you find an item selling for $30 and you can purchase it for $3, you may want to consider it. However if you find there are 250 people on eBay trying to sell the same item, chances are you will not make a quick profit. This is okay for some people and you have to decide how long you are willing to let the item sit before you want to make profit from it.

Chapter 2
Easy to Find Items You Can Make a Profit on

In this chapter I want to continue giving you lots of items you can find at thrift stores and resell on eBay and Amazon for a profit, but I want to focus on the easier items that you can find.

Those that don't take a lot of searching but can still bring in a profit. When I am looking for an item to sell, I only look for items that I can sell for at least 5 times what I paid for it. Sometimes I will purchase an item that will not sell for that much if it is something I know will sell fast and is easy to ship.

1. Coffee mugs. This is an item that is so easy to find and so many people overlook it. Keep an eye out for any StarBucks mugs, Disney, Looney Toons or Snoopy mugs. You can usually get these for 25 to 50 cents and sell them for $5 to $25 dollars depending on the condition and the brands.

2. Tupperware. I am not talking about plastic ware that you can purchase at the grocery store or dollar store. I am talking about real Tupperware. Even if you only find one piece you are still going to be able to turn a great profit on it. You can purchase a piece of Tupperware at a thrift store for a couple dollars up to $5 and turn around and sell it for $15-$30 dollars depending on the condition and the size.

3. Pig items. This is another one of those items that makes no sense to me and I can't tell you why they sell but anything pig related sells great on eBay. This was an odd find for me. My mother collected pigs, I bought her some when I was at a thrift store and a week later

someone had stolen them all off of her porch. I went back and got her more and began thinking, if someone wanted them so bad they would steal I bet I could sell them. I listed a pig I purchased for $3 and sold it for $32! Keep your eye out for those PIGS!!

4. Old bottles of perfume are another item you can find at thrift stores. When I say old I mean OLD not just used. You need to look for fancy bottles and it does not matter how much of the perfume is left. Of course, the more perfume that is in the bottle, the more you will be able to charge but most people will pay for just the bottle by itself.

5. Artwork. This is an item that is a little harder to ship but it is definitely worth looking into. You can regularly get a large piece of art for $5-$10 dollars and sell it very quickly. Even if the artist is unknown, keep an eye on the frames. Many people will purchase the artwork just so they can get an antic looking frame.

6. Old magazines are a great seller as well and let's face it, thrift stores are full of these. You can usually get them for 5 to 10 cents and depending on the topic sell them for a lot more. You want to make sure that they are in good condition, all the pages are intact and they are not torn. You should look for rare or odd subjects such as flying airplanes or bowling. You do not want to look for magazines such as national geographic or magazines that you can find anywhere.

7. Fur is an item you have to watch for. You will usually find this in the winter and most thrift stores keep fur coats with the regular coats. Many employees are not trained to spot real fur when they get it in and will generally mark the price very cheap. I recently purchased a full length fur coat in perfect condition for $50 and priced and sold it for $400.

8. Peanuts items are another great seller on eBay. Remember Charlie Brown, Lucy and Snoopy? Any item you can find that is Peanuts will sell quickly, this includes, toys, coloring books that have not been used, bed sheets or blankets.

9. Vintage cookbooks always sell great as well. One in particular is the Betty Crocker cookbooks. You need to avoid the newer ones and the ones that focus on the microwave. If you can find old cookbooks that are in good condition you can usually pick these up for about $1 a piece and sell them for upwards of $20.

Those are the items for this chapter that you can find at thrift stores very easily and sell on eBay for a profit. My tip for this chapter is that you list often. If you only list one item a week your listings will get lost, when someone searches for the items you are selling the items that were posted the most recent will show up first. Make sure you keep your items in the top few search pages.

Chapter 3
What Else Should You Look For?

1. Blank cassette tapes are always a great find because you cannot go out to your local retail stores and find them anymore. There are still people who love using cassette tapes and will pay good money for them. I never purchase cassette tapes unless they are still sealed in the original packaging and you can make more money with them if you can sell them in lots. I recently was able to purchase 10 tapes for $5 total and sold them in a lot for $45. Look for the brands Denon and Maxell.

2. Just like blank cassette tapes, blank VHS tapes are a great find. Again this should be in their original packaging and it is great if you can purchase several over time and sell them as a lot. Since these are outdated media it is very hard for people to get their hands on them, so they are willing to pay quite a bit for them.

3. You should also keep an eye out for blood pressure machines. Now you are not going to get rich selling these, but you can easily make a $15 profit on a blood pressure machine that you paid $5 for. Always double check and make sure it works before purchasing.

4. I already talked about toys but you should really watch for Care Bears. These were very popular in the 80's and are very popular on eBay. If you look in the area where your thrift store keeps the stuffed animals, you can usually find these and purchase them for less than $1. List them on eBay and sell them for $20 or more.

5. Doll house furniture is another specific item you need to watch for. You can sell these piece by piece or you can create a lot of them if you find enough. Purchasing $20 worth of doll house furniture can bring in a $200 profit without any problem. But don't just focus on the furniture, watch for doll house building items such as tiles or shingles. Many people collect these as well.

   Don't purchase entire doll house kits unless you plan on breaking it up and know you can turn a profit. These are very heavy and cause issues when trying to ship them.

6. Another strange item that sells well on eBay is electric pencil sharpeners. Many people look for older models because they are better built than the ones that sell in stores today. If you can find an electric pencil sharpener, you can list it on eBay for $25 and it will sell quickly.

7. Back to the 80's era toys watch for Puff the Magic Dragon. These are rare but when you find them they usually cost less than $1 and sell for about $30. This is another item that sells quickly and you don't have to worry too much about packing it for shipping because there is nothing that will break on it.

8. Did you know that people are always looking for scrabble tiles? You can usually find these in a bag near the games and if you stock up on them you can make a decent amount from them. You can make about $10 for 100 tiles and many thrift stores will just save these for you and give them to you for free, who doesn't want to make a free 10 dollars?

9. Remember the time before there were MP3 players there was a wonderful item called a Walkman? Watch for these while you are out and about in your thrift stores. These are another hot selling item on eBay and

you can usually get them for just a few dollars. Make sure they work and check the battery area to make sure there is no corrosion or old batteries have not been left in it.

10. Old tube radios are a great item to sell as well and they show up so often in thrift stores. Some of these will sell for around $60, others will sell for thousands of dollars. I recently purchased one for $25 and sold it for $200. I had no clue what I was purchasing and had actually bought it for my house, after a bit of research I decided to sell it.

Before you list your items on eBay make sure you do a little bit of research about the item. Try to find out the year it was made, find out what the value of the item is before you list it so you do not lose money. Make sure you clean the item and take a great picture of it. If there is any damage you need to make sure to list that as well.

Chapter 4
Even More Items You Can Resell For Good Money

Before we begin this chapter I want to make a point. You don't need to go out and try to find all of these items all at once. Instead, choose one or two things that you will search for, then just keep your eye out for items that you think will sell. Always check your phone and see if they are selling on eBay. You can do this by searching the completed listings on eBay. If you go out and try to find all of these items you are just going to overwhelm yourself.

1. Ties are an item that you can usually find at most thrift stores and depending on the condition you can usually sell these for a good profit. Now you don't want to purchase your everyday ties, instead you want to watch for the odd ones. Ties that have characters on them like Taz or ties that have odd sayings, these are the ones that sell the fastest and for the most profit.

2. Most books will not sell well on eBay but there are a few that you should watch for. Little House on The Prairie books and Harry Potter books sell great. If you can find an entire collection you will be able to bring in an even larger profit. One thing I like to do is pick up a book here and there when I find them. Once the collection is complete you can sell them for a profit.

3. House décor is so cheap at thrift stores, in fact it is one place that I prefer to buy items to decorate with. This can be items such as flower pots or a center piece for a table, or even fake floral arrangements. You can purchase these for $1-$2 and sell them for at least $10.

You do want to watch the weight of the items though because most people do not want to pay more for shipping than they are for the item itself.

4. Knick Knacks are in abundance at thrift stores and sell for about a quarter a piece max. If you can purchase an entire collection of them and sell them as a lot you will make a huge profit. Spending just $2.50 can bring you a $20 profit with no problems.

5. Old Christmas lights are an item that many people overlook but can be sold on eBay for a profit! By old I do not mean 2 or 3 years old, I mean Christmas lights from the 50's or 60's. You can get about $40 for just one strand of these lights. Always check to make sure the lights are working before purchasing.

6. Cast iron skillets will bring in a huge profit as well. I recently found a set of four skillets for $7 at a local thrift store. I took them home, cleaned them up and sold the entire set for $134. These have to be vintage cast iron and you will have to know how to clean them up if you want to sell them. If you know how to clean and season cast iron there is a lot of money to be made.

7. Vintage cake decorating books will sell for a huge profit as well. You need to make sure they are in good condition but a $1 investment can bring you $45 in profit.

When you are in thrift stores looking for your items, shop like it is your job because it is. Don't look at this as a hobby because if you do you will not be successful. I am not saying that you should not take risks but you need to be careful in doing so.

Chapter 5
Unique Items You Never Thought
Would Sell

1. Two colored golf balls are another item that seems
   strange but sells like crazy on eBay. I have seen some of
   these balls go for over $60 with an investment of only
   $1-$2.

2. While you are digging around the clothes in your thrift
   shop keep an eye out for square dancing items. Many of
   these will sell very quickly on eBay. Most of the time
   you can get a square dancing dress for $8 at a thrift
   store and sell it for $80 or more on eBay.

3. 8 track players!!! This is an item that I see all the time
   and can usually get for $5-$10 and sell for a couple
   hundred on eBay. You need to know a little bit about
   them so make sure you do your research before you
   purchase any. You need to make sure they work as well
   but these are an amazing find.

4. This brings me to my next item which is 8 tracks. Just
   like cassette tapes these are going to sell quickly and
   you can make a great profit off of them. Unlike cassette
   tapes you will need to pay attention to what is on the
   tracks. A random track of someone speaking is not
   going to sell you need to know a little bit about music to
   make this work.

5. You should also watch for old records and record
   players. You can find record players for about $10-$20
   and sell them for close to $100 and you can find records
   for about $1 a piece. I like to keep a record collector
   guide with me while looking at records. This way I can

quickly refer to the guide and know whether the record is going to be profitable or not.

6. Old bamboo fishing rods will bring in a great profit as well. It is amazing when you purchase an old fishing rod for a couple of dollars and turn around and sell it for $50-$150. Your profit will depend on the length of the rod and the condition of it but you can guarantee this will sell very quickly.

Once you have been going to thrift stores for a little while, don't be afraid to branch out a little bit and shop at flea markets or estate sales as well. Most of the items in this book can be found in these places just as easily as they are found in thrift stores and sometimes it is easier to find them at the flea market or estate sales. Just make sure you do not end up paying more for an item than you would at a thrift store. Keep your profit in mind during all of your purchases.

Chapter 6

Some 1980's Items You Can Sell and Make Profit On

1. Remember how popular My Little Pony was back in the 80's? Well guess what, it is just as popular now with a bit of a higher price tag. I have sold lots of 50 My Little Pony's for well over $200. This was about a $25 investment so anytime you see them make sure you grab them and put them away until you have a nice little stash.

2. Have you ever known that person who had an entire room full of Hot Wheels still in the package or Star Wars figurines? Well guess what, these people are willing to pay a ton of money for these and you can find them at thrift stores! Keep an eye out for anything that was made pre 90's and has the packaging in good condition.

3. Smurfs are another item you need to keep your eyes peeled for. It does not matter if what you find is the small plastic Smurfs, the stuffed ones or even if it is bed sheets. I sold one Smurfette bed set sell for over $50. The only thing you need to watch is that you are not trying to sell the new Smurfs as the old ones. Look at the tag and make sure otherwise you will have some very unhappy customers.

4. As you can see there is a lot of money in different types of toys, another item to watch for is old Winchester toy

guns. Most of these are cap guns and can bring in up to $50 each depending on the condition of the gun.

5. Military items sell quickly as well, watch for anything from WW2 or earlier, helmets, uniforms literally everything sells.

Remember to watch for things you don't see often when you are shopping. Many people will see items such as a bread maker priced at $2 and think they can turn a huge profit, but look at how many bread makers are on the shelf. 5, 10 maybe 15 even. Watch for the rare, not the items you know the thrift store will have every time you go in.

Chapter 7

The Odd Selling Items That Sell Great

In this chapter I want to give you a few items that you can find literally everywhere and still make a profit from them on eBay. I am not going to pretend I know why these items sell, who buys these items or what use anyone has for these items. I am however going to warn you that these are quite strange but you can still make a profit off of them.

1. Pine cones. If you find a box of pine cones lying around a thrift store, you can list them on eBay and sell them for $30. Find an extra large pine cone and get $30 out of it all by itself. If you can't find these in a thrift store, grab a bag and start searching for them. Pine cones equal big money.

2. Vintage stickers can bring in some big time money. Look in your thrift store in the knick knack section. I once found a bag full of 1980's skateboard stickers for $5. They threw 100's of original 1980's skateboard stickers in 1 bag. I sold the same Vision Street Wear and Powell Peralta 1980's vintage skateboard stickers over and over for years at $10 a piece.

3. Altoids candy tins are another item people go crazy for. These do need to be vintage, but are super easy to find at thrift stores and most of the time they will just give them to you, but don't be fooled some of these sell for several hundred dollars each.

4. Vintage synthesizers. Always keep your eyes peeled for vintage synthesizers like the Moog and Roland Juno 106. Usually the thrift store does not know the

difference from a cheap little Casio keyboard and a truly vintage synthesizer. Basically as a rule of thumb, the more knobs the synthesizer has, the better. I bought a Roland Juno 106 at a thrift store for $20 and resold it on eBay for over $500.

5. The last item I have for you is your egg cartons. When you buy a dozen eggs in those foam like cartons, save them farmers will purchase them from you, you can get about $10-$15 dollars for 40 of them and all you have to do is eat your eggs.

Those are the 50 items that you can purchase at a low cost and sell on eBay for a profit, but before I finish up this book I want to give you a few tips that you can use while you look for items.

First don't feel like you need to stick to what I have told you in this book. When I first started out, I would pick up an item and ask myself would I purchase this for myself, would anyone I know purchase it, if I could answer yes to either question and the item was cheap enough I got it.

You should also try to shop in high end areas. So many people would rather donate to thrift stores instead of having a yard sale or selling their items on eBay. If you want to get high end items you need to shop in thrift stores that are in high end areas. This is especially helpful when you are looking for name brand clothing or fur. One warning though, most of these thrift stores know their items are high end and will charge more than other thrift stores.

You need to make sure you take a few items with you. You should always have a smart phone. You also need to make sure you take a few batteries with you when you are shopping. If you are looking for a Walkman you need to take a cassette with you that you know works as well as a pair of headphones.

Keep some anti-bacterial lotion wipes with you as well, you are going to be going through a lot of items, many of these are dirty or dusty, and they have been handled by many other people. You will want to not only keep your hands clean but germ free as well.

Another tip is that you should get to know the people who work in the stores you shop at the most. This can be a huge asset. If you take a few minutes and get to know them, they tend to let you know if they have come across great donations. Some will even call you and let you know something great has been put out on a shelf. Some will even hold items back for you!

Thrift stores have days where different items are on sale. Sometimes there may be a bag sale where you can purchase an entire bag of clothing for only a few dollars. Sometimes electronics will be on sale and so forth, you get the idea. These are the days you want to shop and really stock up on product. You can also shop at the end of season sales if you don't mind holding on to your product for a little while before turning a profit. This also requires some storage space as well so it is not for everyone.

Plan a schedule and stick to it! I can't stress this enough. If you really are serious about making money from flipping thrift shop items, you need to make a plan and stick to it. This means finding out which stores are your favorite and visiting them every week. Listing your items without procrastinating and shipping as soon as payments are approved.

You can make money by flipping thrift shop items on eBay, but it is going to take work. There are going to be times that you are going to fail. Some months you will make more sales than others and some months you may not see any profit at all but that does not mean you should give up. Instead learn from the experience, figure out what you are doing wrong and move on.

Shop early in the morning, most thrift shops restock overnight although some will stock the shelves on Monday so you should shop early in the week and early in the day. You will find the best items this way instead of having to choose what others have already picked through.

Have a system as well. Make a plan for going through each thrift store. For example, start with the clothing, then the shoes, electronics, move on going through each area of the store. Without a plan it can be very overwhelming and you will end up focusing on the stress instead of focusing on finding great items to sell.

I know the items in this last chapter were a little odd but I did that for a reason. The truth is almost anything will sell on eBay if you are willing to wait for the right buyer to come along. Sometimes this means your items will fly off of your shelves and other times it means the items will sit for a long time. However, if you focus on what I have told you in this book and use the tips I have given you, your items will sell quickly.

I hope that you enjoy flipping thrift store items!!!

Conclusion

I hope this book was able to help you to start learning how to flip thrift store items and sell them on eBay.

The next step is to head out to the thrift store and see what you can find.

Finally, if you enjoyed this book, then I'd like to ask you for a favor, would you be kind enough to leave a review for this book on Amazon? It'd be greatly appreciated!

Made in the USA
Middletown, DE
20 January 2024

48211418R00170